William Echard Golden

A Brief History of the English Drama from the Earliest to the Latest

Times

William Echard Golden

A Brief History of the English Drama from the Earliest to the Latest Times

ISBN/EAN: 9783337304218

Printed in Europe, USA, Canada, Australia, Japan

Cover: Foto ©ninafisch / pixelio.de

More available books at **www.hansebooks.com**

A BRIEF HISTORY

OF THE

ENGLISH DRAMA

From the Earliest to the Latest Times

BY

WILLIAM ECHARD GOLDEN, A. M.

NEW YORK

WELCH, FRACKER COMPANY

1890

———————

PREFACE.

The treatment of a subject of such extent and importance as the one I have chosen, is beset with many and peculiar difficulties. These, during several years' careful study, I have endeavored to overcome. How successful I have been, must be left for my readers to decide. My object has been to give as concise an historical and literary account of the drama, its origin, development and present status as may be embraced in a brief course of lectures. I have necessarily consulted many works of reference and taken copious notes. I am also indebted for suggestions to Dr. A. V. W. Jackson, of Columbia College, and Professor O. B. Clark, of Indiana University.

W. E. GOLDEN.

LECTURES.

THE ENGLISH DRAMA.

I.

THE MYSTERY, MIRACLE AND MORAL PLAYS.

In the early part of this century Thomas Sharp, editing a treatise on the Coventry Mystery Plays, had occasion to remark, in the introduction to his work, that while the history of the English Stage had been investigated with a perseverance and minuteness of research that scarcely left any expectation of additional facts remaining undiscovered, our Religious Dramas or Mysteries, the unquestionable groundwork of the Stage, had been treated in a very superficial and unsatisfactory manner.

That Mr. Sharp was right in his statement
then is undoubted, but I do not believe it is so
applicable at present. Since his book appeared, and doubtless partly owing to its appearance, a great deal of careful labor and
investigation has been expended on this comparatively unworked field of English literature. Ward has written his history ; Lucy
Toulman Smith has edited the York Plays.

There are three grand classes or kinds of
poetry : the lyric, the epic, the dramatic.
And of these the dramatic is the highest, for
it is not only a different class, but it may also
include either or both of the others.

Song is a primary mode of expression for
the emotion. Hence it is common, in one
form or another, in some degree of excellence, to nearly all, if not to all, peoples.

A connected narrative exacts, however, a
higher order of intellect than is necessary for
the appreciation and understanding of a song.
Attention is required. The powers of comparison, of judgment, of reflection are called
into use. All persons are not capable of this.
Therefore, that which appeals to a higher
order of mind for comprehension must necessarily belong to a higher class of work.

There are nations that have been capable

of the production and appreciation of the song and the narrative, that is to say, of lyric and epic poetry; but there are no nations that have not reached a certain intellectual development that have produced the last and highest form of poetry, the dramatic. I do not include in this rather sweeping assertion the peoples who, by religious conviction, not by intellectual incompetence, have been restrained from production in this department.

The powers of abstract thought necessary for the conception, even more than the comprehension of the dramatic form, denotes a certain stage of civilization that need not be demanded by either the lyric or epic. A savage can feel a song, can understand a story. To comprehend a play something more is necessary.

I would have it understood that I am speaking of these poetical forms as being in their simplest undeveloped state. I make no assertions of the highly perfected productions the best age of literature has produced, except this, to name the primal and eternal order of poetical work.

There have been three great dramatic epochs: viz., the Greek, the Spanish and the

English. It is only with the last of these
that we are concerned.

Undisputedly the modern drama, of which
the English is a branch, sprang not from the
domain of literature but from religious
worship.

It has been claimed that the modern is an
offspring of the ancient drama. This is in no
sense the truth. There are links of connection between the two, but one did not origin-
ate in the other. Indeed, if the origin of the
Greek drama itself be sought for, it will be
found, as is that of the modern, in religious
worship.

Returning to the modern drama, and seek-
ing for the direct occasion of its ontgrowth,
we shall find that the best authorities are
agreed that the idea was first conceived, and
the comprehension first acquired of the play,
by the liturgy of the mass. "That," says
Ward, "is the original mystery."

The liturgy of the mass is a service, familiar
to all Roman Catholics, performed by an individual, or association of individuals, on be-
half of the community. This is a public performance of a religious office of paramount
importance. It includes the Confession of
sins, the *Credo, Agnus Dei*, etc., etc.

If any one has ever been in a Catholic church during such a service, he will readily perceive that it is really a sacred performance. The priests in their robes, the illusions of vestments and ornaments, the responses of the congregation, all go to imprint a dramatic stamp upon the service.

It is not remarkable then that from the church service should spring a means by which the *vulgus* should be instructed and amused, nor that the priests should be the first to produce this means.

Few in early times could read. The Bibles, for a long period, were in Latin only. Books were very rare, and very valuable. During the middle ages, the higher aspirations, emotions and ideas of the people were clustered around the church. In their religious worship alone did they find the expression of their spiritual natures. In the stories of the Bible, and later of the saints, therefore, they felt the deepest interest.

Realizing the neccessity of satisfying in some degree and in their own way this want of the people, and also to oppose the plays of the Gentiles and to supersede the profane dancing, music, etc., at the ancient fairs, the priests arranged the Scriptural stories in a form that could at once instruct and interest their flocks.

Voltaire says that Gregory Nazianzen wrote in the fourth century his play of Christ's Passion, and others of the same kind, in order to oppose the dramatic works of the ancient Greeks and Romans. There seems little reason to doubt this.

Certain it is that Hroswitha, the Benedictine nun of Gandersheim, wrote sacred plays in the tenth century, to counteract the effect of the plays of Terence. She even took her antagonist's works as a model for her own.

In 1119 the Mystery-play of St. Katharine was presented at Dunstaple under the direction of a monk named Geoffrey. This kind of production was common in London before the close of the century. The plays were written at first in Latin and French, and it was not until the reign of Edward III. that they were permanently succeeded by English versions.

Collier says that no country of Europe, since the revival of letters, has been able to produce any notice of theatrical performances of so early a date as England. And the love of the drama seems ever since to have been characteristic of the people of England and their descendants.

The oldest form of dramatic composition in our language is the Mystery Play. Concerning these early compositions there has been considerable confusion as to the different classes into which they should be arranged, and the proper nomenclature applicable to these classes. At the time that they were written and performed, no distinction was made, and none was probably thought of. They were all plays. Ward and other leading authorities have made, however, three divisions of these early works, which I shall accept.

The first dramatic compositions, extending over some three hundred years, and after the appearance of the drama in its present form, we shall treat of under three heads, viz.: the Mystery Plays, the Miracle Plays, the Moral Plays.

The Mystery Plays deal only with Scriptural passages, stories from the Bible.

The Miracle Plays deal with legends concerning saints of the church.

The Moral Plays deal with allegory.

The earliest of these three classes to appear was, as I have said, the Mystery Play. Accepting the theory that from religious worship, from the liturgy immediately, the drama was derived, the first subjects to be treated of we would naturally look for in the Scriptures. And we would find them there.

A number of isolated plays treating of some one biblical story exists ; as *Parfre's Candel-mas-Day*, which treats of the massacre of the innocents, and the flight into Egypt, the *Conversion of Saul*, and *Mary Magdalene.* This last is the most remarkable and most elaborate of the single plays.

Until within the last few years, in fact as late as the publication of Ward's History of English Dramatic Literature, it has been usual to assert that there were but three connected series of Mystery Plays. But the publication of a MSS. in the library of Lord Ashburnham, edited by Lucy Toulman Smith, has added one more series to this list. This very valuable contribution includes the York Plays.

It is not a little remarkable that these plays had never yet seen the light. Scholars have known since Thoresby's History of Leeds was published that such a collection existed ; but no one before Lucy T. Smith seems to have more than hastily glanced at them.

The history of the volume is curious. It was the book wherein the plays, performed by the crafts from the fourteenth to the sixteenth centuries, with the sanction and authority of the corporation, were " registered " by the city officers and it must therefore have belonged to the corporation. It was at one time in the care of the priory of Holy Trinity, in Micklegate. At the time of the Reformation various attempts were made to amend the book of plays, as is shown both by many notes scattered through its leaves and by notices in the municipal records ; but in spite of these the plays ceased to be performed about 1580, not being able to withstand the spirit of the times. What now became of the book is doubtful. Until 1579 at least it remained in the possession of the city. Later it is known to have passed into the hands of the Fairfax family. In 1695 Ralph Thoresby owned it and at the sale of Thoresby's collection, in 1764, Horace Walpole bought it for £1 1s. At Walpole's sale Thomas Rodd, a bookseller, gave £220 10s., and sold it to Mr. Heywood Bright, of Bristol, in 1842, for £235. At the dispersion of this gentleman's collection, in 1844, Mr. Thorp bought it for £305 for the Rev. Thomas Russell, and it was afterwards sold to the late Earl of Ashburnham.

This valuable book consists of two hundred and seventy leaves of parchment, forty-eight of which are blank. It is bound in the original wooden binding, once covered with leather, which is now much torn and in rather bad condition. The blank pages at the beginning and end have been nibbled by mice. Scattered through the volume are frequent small alterations, or corrections.

A series of Mystery Plays, as the phrase is here used, means a number of plays that, taking up the Bible story with the creation or before, carry it through the sacred narrative and even to doomsday. Of such series there are four, viz.:

    1. The Chester Plays.
    2. The Coventry Plays.
    3. The Towneley Plays.
    4. The York Plays.

These are by no means all the series that were produced, but they are all that remain.

Mystery Plays are recorded to have been given at Dunstaple, London, Cambridge, Canterbury, Winchester, Worcester, Sleaford, Reading, Lincoln, Shrewsbury, Witney, Preston, Lancaster, Kendall, Beverly, Wakefield, New-Castle-on-Tyne, Leicester, Edinburgh, Heybridge, Dublin, etc., etc. Indeed, they were common all over the kingdom.

It is incredible that out of all these places only four should have produced a series of plays. Yet it is not to be denied that the celebrity of the four preserved far exceeds that of those which are lost, and may in part account for their preservation.

The authorship of these plays cannot, with any degree of certainty, be accredited to any one man in any known instance. They are rather to be taken as the work of many men at many times. A play was, without doubt, rewritten when emergency demanded. Or it may have been separated into two or more plays. On the other hand, several plays were combined into one at times. The reasons for these alterations are apparent.

Although the Mystery Plays were originally written and, perhaps, represented by priests, in course of time, partly on account of the disapproval of the high ecclesiastical authorities, partly on account of other difficulties, the presentations passed into the hands of the common people ; that is, the city guilds or trades.

When the performances came to be held, each guild had assigned to it, as its own play, some part of the Scriptures. The guilds gave their plays in succession, so that the guild which had for its subject the Creation, should first perform, and the guild whose subject was Doomsday, should be the last to be seen. By this means the whole story of the Bible was narrated.

But the number of guilds was not always the same. Trades arise from necessity, and from lack of necessity disappear. When armor ceased to be worn, armor making ceased to be a trade. With the abandonment of the bow and arrow went the Fletchers and Bowmen. In our own time we have seen old trades vanish and many new ones appear.

Now, however the number of guilds varied, the story remained the same. Hence it was necessary, at times, to combine, at other times to separate the plays. Also it is to be noted that, while it was usual for each guild to have its play, yet it is quite common for several guilds to unite in the presentation of a play.

The CHESTER PLAYS, twenty-five of which remain, were annually performed, with some interruptions, from 1268 to 1577, at Chester, England. The plays, as was usual, took their name from the place in which they were given. The authorship has been assigned by some to Ralph Higden. But this is improbable, though he may have contributed towards

their production. They were given beginning Whit-Monday and continuing until
Wednesday. Of these plays there are two
manuscripts in the British Museum ; the
earlier dated 1600 and the other 1607. The
plays are unequal in merit. They follow the
text of the Gospel very closely and contain
but little legendary matter. The lamenta-
tion of Mary, which occurs in these plays, is
a common subject of English verse in manuscripts of various dates. One or two short examples will be found in the *Reliquiæ Antiquæ.*
Another popular character of the mediæval
religious literature is Longius, the blind
knight, who pierced the side of the Saviour
with his spear, and recovered his sight by the
water that trickled from the wound on his
eye. Although containing comparatively little legendary matter, as has been remarked,
yet, in the Chester Plays, as in the other series
of Mysteries, there are to be found plays that
are, strictly speaking, Miracles ; as " *The
Harrowing of Hell,*" the eighteenth play.
The legend which forms the subject of this
play, so very popular in the middle ages, was
taken from the apocryphal Gospel of Nico-
demus. It forms a separate play in the
Towneley and Coventry series, though in the

latter it is very brief. The twenty-second play, "*Ezechiel*," appears to be peculiar to the Chester collection, and is a curious specimen of the manner in which the Gospel was expounded to the vulgar.

LUDUS COVENTRIÆ, the Coventry plays, forty-two in all, were presented during the fifteenth and sixteenth centuries at Coventry. They were acted at other places also. The MSS. was written at least as early as the reign of Henry VII., and is now preserved in the Cottonian collection of MSS. Its history is wrapped in obscurity. The Coventry Mysteries were performed on the feast of Corpus Christi, the favorite time for such exhibitions in England. They acquired considerable celebrity and attracted immense multitudes to the city. Even royalty visited the town in order to witness the plays. In 1486 Henry VII. was present at the performance on St. Peter's day, and in 1492 he again attended, and this time with his queen.

The TOWNELEY PLAYS number thirty-two. They take their name from the circumstance that the MSS. in which they have been preserved formed part of the library in Towneley Hall, Lancashire. Their composition is probably due to the Friars of Woodkirk or Nostel.

Being written in the dialect of the district in which they were acted, and containing a large number of Scandinavian words, they are quite difficult to read. The MSS. appears to date from about the reign of Henry VI.

The YORK PLAYS, as enumerated in *Liber diversorum memorandum civitatem ebor targentium*, one of the oldest books that the city of York now possesses, in 1415 numbered fifty-one. In the second list fifty-seven plays are named. Lord Ashburnham's MSS. contains forty-eight. These plays, on examination, are found to correspond more to the first than the second list. .The probable date of the MSS., such as that of all of the mysteries, is between 1430–1440. The date of the authorship is very much earlier ; it may be a century. Both internal and external evidence point to this fact. Reference is made to these plays in 1378, and again in 1394, as belonging to the old time. The internal evidences are the metre and style. There is much skill in versification shown. Rhyme and alliteration both are used. The language is in a stage of transition. The York Plays, sometimes called Corpus Christi Plays, from the time at which they were given, continued to be played until 1568. Then the church interfered, and

although strenuous efforts were made to
change the opinions of the clergy, they were
unsuccessful, for before 1600 the performances
of the "York Mysteries" were discontinued.
The characteristics of these plays were : clear-
ness and precision in the narrative, adherence
to the Bible story, simplicity, directness and
completion of plan.   They compare favorably
in diction and verse with the better specimens
of Middle English Northern poetry. The
York cycle forms an important contribution,
for it is as a whole the most complete collection.   It is free from much of the coarse fun
and "groundling" incident which were introduced into the Coventry and Towneley plays.
The last named are written in the same dialect as the York cycle, and five of them are
the same as five of the York Plays, with certain passages cut out or modified.

The place of exhibition was sometimes a
church, sometimes the halls of corporations,
but most frequently the open street. The
street was preferred because greater multitudes could be accommodated, and also to
suit the peculiar manner in which the plays
were represented.

The plays were divided according to the
trades-guilds of the city. Each play was

given by one or more corporations, which furnished and brought forth a vehicle to be used as a movable stage. These vehicles usually consisted of two platforms, one above the other. The one above was open and was where the play was given. The lower one was closed, generally with curtains, and served as a dressing place for the actors. It is said that this lower room was often used to represent hell, and the devils always issued forth or were consigned to this lower room as their abode. A third platform above the other two was sometimes used to represent heaven. This platform, however, was not common to the " English·Mysteries." Riccobini, in his history of the French stage, says that in France the theatre showed paradise, heaven, hell and the earth all at once. From which we infer that the triple or quadruple platform was peculiar rather to the " French Mysteries" than to those of England. In later days we have borrowed something else from the French pertaining to these early plays, viz. : the appellation "Mysteries." They were not so called in England, but in France the name was always given. The vehicles, in both countries, upon which the plays were given were movable, being either

on four or six wheels, and usually were drawn
by men. This moving about was accompanied with great difficulty, owing to the
rude construction of the vehicles.

In York the order of procedure was as follows : In solemn procession, one vehicle after
the other, first at the great gates of the
Priory of the Holy Trinity ; next to the Cathe-
dral Church of York, afterwards to the Hospi-
tal of St. Leonard, etc., etc. The procession was preceded by a vast number of
lighted torches, and a great multitude of
priests in their proper habits, followed by
the mayor and the citizens, with a prodigious
crowd of the populace attending.

Originally each vehicle was called a pageant. Afterwards the word pageant came to
imply the show as well as the stage. Finally
it was applied to the whole series of shows
whence the modern meaning. As used in the
following account of an exhibition of the Coventry Plays the word evidently means the
individual plays.

" The place where they played them was in
every street. They began first at the Abay
gates, and when the first pagiante was played,
it was wheeled to the high cross before the
mayor, and soe to every street, and soe every

street had a pagiante playing before them at one time, till all the pagiantes for the day appointed were played, and when one pagiante was near ended, word was brought from street to street, that soe they might come in place thereof, exceeding orderlye, and all the streets have their pagiantes afore them all at one time playing togeather."

Some details of these performances and their appurtenances will not be uninteresting.

Music was furnished by men called minstrels or waits, according as to whether they were employed for the pagiantes or by the city. These musicians had silver badges and chains provided at the expense of the city. It appears that the musicians, being employed chiefly in processions and other open air exhibitions, used wind-instruments, such as pipes, bag-pipes, trumpets, etc.

At Coventry a person was appointed "dresser" of each pageant. In the course of the performance ale was given to the players, and in the Smith's pageant Pilate, being a principal personage, was allowed wine.

In the list of machinery used in the Draper's pageant there is included :

A Hell-mouth (a fire kept in it).

An Earthquake.

A Link to set the world on fire.

Pulpits for the angels.

How the effects were produced is not however very clearly explained.

Amongst the characters of one play are named "Two Worms of Conscience."

Banner bearers proclaimed the argument of each pageant. Usually these men were styled Vexillatores, but in Chester they were known as Banes or Banns.

Besides the Corpus Christi and Whitsuntide plays, there were other pageants as that of Hoke-Tuesday or Hoke-Tide, and also for particular occasions, as in 1416, when Parliament was held in the Priory at Coventry, and again in 1455, when Queen Margaret visited the city.

In the Religious Mysteries the devil was a favorite and very prominent character. In the Miracle and Moral plays he is likewise found. In the latter he has a constant attendant called Vice, who was always the buffoon of the piece. The devil was usually represented with a very wide mouth, staring eyes, a large nose, a red beard, cloven feet, and a tail.

Judas, in accordance with the popular belief, was represented always with red hair and beard.

The fiends were often exhibited as carrying the sins and souls of men in sacks.

Many of these plays are reported to have been very indelicate. Nevertheless, they were not without their use, for they both impressed on the rude minds of the unlettered people the chief facts of their religion and softened manners, which were at that time very gross and impure. " They created insensibly," says Mr. Warton, "a regard for other arts than those of bodily strength and savage valor."

The Passion Play of Ober Ammergau enables us at the present time to understand the effect produced by the Mysteries and Miracles upon a mediæval audience.

As change is the inevitable law of nature in all things, its force is perceivable in the drama as elsewhere. First the mere biblical narrative satisfied writer and auditor, as in the Mysteries. In time the legends of saints were drawn upon for topics on which plays might be written, and we have the Miracle Plays. Next symbolical characters, which had long held some part in both Mystery and Miracle Plays, began to absorb the whole action, and the Moral Play appeared.

The Moral Play, we have said, deals with allegory. That is to say, its characters are symbolical, and its purpose is to teach men to live better lives. Early in the fifteenth century this species of the drama appeared, and though the Mystery Plays continued to be given, their popularity waned perceptibly before their younger rivals.

The transition from the Mysteries and Miracles to the Moralities, was expedited by their being no essential difference in the mode of performance. The same vehicles, or the same kind, served for the use of the last as it had for that of the two preceding phases. However, they came to be acted by roving companies on holidays and festivals, in the halls of noblemen and gentry, as well as in the open squares of towns. They acquired the subordinate name of Interlude from the custom of presenting them in the intervals of . banquets or of other pastimes.

It is probable that literary allegory and the popularity of the Moralities in France, gave rise to the Moralities in England. But however successful in Gaul, they never domesticated themselves in Britain until they came to be connected with the political and religious questions which agitated the nation at large, as they did during the Reformation of Henry VIII.

The Moralities were composed during the uncertain reigns of the first three Tudors. Hence they reflect the conflict of opinion between Protestantism and the older faith. Some satirize bitterly the Protestants, some the Catholics.

Two characters that were prominent in one form or another in the Moral Plays were the devil and his attendant, Vice. This latter character was not derived from the French, whatever else the Moralities may owe to that source, but was of native origin. There is no French equivalent. Vice appears under many different names, such as Shift, Ambidexter, Sin, Fraud, Iniquity, etc. He was usually dressed in a fool's habit. Later the character was blended with the domestic fool, and as such has survived in the regular drama. With Vice the idea of comedy in the English drama was first born.

A list of Moral Plays, belonging to the reign of Henry VII., is interesting, if only for their names, which suggest the style of piece represented.

1. The Castle of Perseverance.
2. Mankind.
3. Nature.
4. The World and the Child.

5. Mind, Will and Understanding.
6. Everyman.
7. *Lusty Juventus.*

It will be well to take one of these and examine the story, that we may the better understand the nature of the whole class. We will take " The Castle of Perseverance."

The subject of "The Castle of Persever-ance" is the warfare carried on against *Humanum Genus* and his companions, the Seven Cardinal Virtues, by the Seven Deadly Sins and their commanders, *Mundus, Belial* and *Caro*.   He is besieged by them in the Castle of Perseverance, where *Confessio* has bidden him take up his abode.   In his old age he finally gives way to the persuasions of *Avaritia*.   His soul is at last arraigned by *Pater sedens in judicio,* but is apparently saved.

This is the type of conflict between good and bad in man, as represented in the Moral Plays.   This class of plays survived to the close of the sixteenth and even into the first years of the seventeenth century.   But al-ready in the early period efforts had been made to disengage the Moral Play from its allegorical setting, and to present the pith of its motives in a form of comedy.   The law of change was active and showed itself in an intermixture of abstract and real personages, then of a division into acts and scenes as in " The Marriage of Witte and Reason," and finally the abstract was entirely dispensed with, the acts and scenes entirely adopted, and our Comedy proper appeared.

Stephen Hawe's " Pastime of. Pleasure " (temp. Henry VIII.) was the last work of the old school of allegory in the pre-Elizabethan literature.

Amongst the most celebrated writers of Moral Plays we may name Guillaume Herman, Etienne Langton and John Skelton.

II.

THE PREDECESSORS OF SHAKESPEARE.

DRAMATIC literature is that kind of composition which adjusts itself to the requirements of the imitative art, acting. When the requirements of the imitative art are fully met without detraction from the value of the composition, the highest object of dramatic literature has been attained. But this perfect union of poetry and action is not brought about in a day. With the drama it required centuries. Nor in the limits of this lecture do we treat of the perfection afterwards attained. Here it shall be our desire to observe the development of the play to trace through the several stages that literary activity which was to make the Shakespearean drama possible. Between the liturgy and "Hamlet" lies an apparently impassible gulf. It would be ridiculous to suppose that the one immediately proceeded from the other. It is only when we fill in the intervening gap with the Mysteries, Miracles and Moralities, when we remark how the religious element at first all-predominant and all pervading is gradually eliminated, and how worldly objects and personages little by little supplant and finally exclude it, that we begin to perceive the connection. When the Mystery Play appeared, the idea of religious worship pertaining to the liturgy was lost. With the introduction of the Miracle Play there was a slight but still more perceptible deviation in proportion as the events and personages ceased to be scriptural and became legendary. In the composition of the Moral Plays the religious idea was merged into that of the moral as sacred characters were into allegorical. But from the earliest times there were those who endeavored to seize upon the substance of the Moral Play, and dispensing with allegorical accompaniments mould it into the form of Comedy or Tragedy.

Midway between the Moralities and the drama proper we find three works representative of the struggle to free the play from allegory. These three compositions, Bale's "King Johan," "Appius and Virginia" and "Cambyses," have been appropriately styled *Hybrids*, which name I shall adopt. Partly moralities and partly tragedies, the *Hybrids*

are chiefly interesting as illustrations of
dramatic evolution. "King Johan" is deserving, probably, of special mention, as it is the
first attempt in the language to dramatize the
Chronicles, and might be placed with considerable propriety at the head of a list com-
prising what afterwards came to be known as
Chronicle Plays. "Appius and Virginia"
treats in a very crude manner the well-known
story of the Roman maiden. "Cambyses,"
the Eastern tyrant, furnishes the subject for
the third play. The poetry of these pieces is
sing-song and puerile, indicative of its
infancy.

Contemporaneously with the later Moralities appeared a peculiarly English phase of
the drama ; the Interlude. This type, the
invention of John Heywood, on account of
its wit and humor, shines forth pleasantly
from all the wearisome literature of the
Moralities. It deserves, then, some special
treatment from the pen of a grateful student.

An interlude is a dialogue, mirthful, without intrigue, exhibiting characters not by
action but by contrast and arrangement, the
motive of which is furnished by a witty situation. Sometimes it partook of the character
of a Morality, as in " The Play of the Weather "

and " The Play of Love." As a rule, however, it corresponded in form to the Latin
Disputationes. Some few pieces, as " The
Four P's," constitute a separate class. This
phase of dramatic evolution was not destined
long to continue. In a few years the Interludes became almost as archaic as they are at
the present day. Other influences were to
produce a different type which should forever replace the Interlude. At the time of
their composition no equally artistic dramatic
works existed.

John Heywood, the originator of the Interlude, was a Londoner, a graduate of Broad-
gate Hall, now Pembroke College, Oxford.
He was a staunch Catholic and a fierce opponent of the Reformed Church. During
Henry the Eighth's and Mary's reigns he was
in high favor at Court, but died in exile at
Mechlin in 1565. Despite his zeal and sufferings for his faith, he was not blind to the corruption of the church. This he bitterly satirized and fearlessly exposed. His literary
style is homely, sensible, shrewd and witty.
His writings belong to the first half of the
sixteenth century.

When to Heywood's faculty of character
painting was added the power of construct-

ing a story, a plot, we have the essential elements for the production of comedy. From the Moralities, through the aid of the Interludes and the examples furnished by the Latin and Italian dramatists, comedy emerged. As the story became prominent and began to share the interest with the study of character, Comedy differentiated into that of character and that of incident, which latter is the higher as well as the later development.

The earliest regular comedy in the English language, an honor long mistakenly attributed to "Gammer Gurton's Needle," is Nicholas Udall's "Ralph Roister Doister." The only known early copy of this comedy is in the library of Eton College, from which have been printed at different times of late years numerous editions. The play was licensed and probably first printed in 1566, but is supposed to have been composed and performed even before 1551, in which year it is quoted in Wilson's "Rule of Reason."

"Ralph Roister Doister," written by a scholar and schoolman, shows the influence of classic models both in the construction of a plot and in the handling and division of the subject. In this play we leave the grotesqueness and allegory of the middle ages and enter into the field of actual and natural life. The comedy founded on Plautus' "*Miles Gloriosus*," has for its story the courtship and rejection of a cowardly, vain-glorious braggart, who gives his name to the piece. None of the requisite components of comedy are wanting, such as ridiculous and serious personages, amusing events, misunderstandings, temporary perplexity and a final satisfactory adjustment of everything. As regards the general plan and spirit of the work it differs little from many modern works of mediocrity, and with revision might be as suitable for representation.

Nicholas Udall, the author of "Ralph Roister Doister," born about 1505, in Hampshire, was a Protestant. He was a student at Oxford and afterwards headmaster at Eton College and later of Westminster School. He was a man of learning and gained considerable fame by translating some of Erasmus' Latin Paraphrases of the New Testament. Udall died in 1556.

Some fifteen or twenty years after the production of "Ralph Roister Doister," that is to say, in 1566, a vastly inferior work, John Still's "Gammer Gurton's Needle," was

played in Christ College, Cambridge. A
comedy in five acts (it might better be termed
an elaborated farce). It is built on the circumstance of an old woman losing her needle,
the whole village being thrown into confusion in consequence, and the final discovery of
the missing needle in the seat of her servant's
trousers. Needles do not appear to have
been very plentiful at the time, if we may
judge from the disturbance caused by the
loss of this one. The piece is coarse and
vulgar, but humorous and vigorous. The
existence of " Ralph Roister Doister," in
every way a much better work, does not
seem to have at all affected " Gammer Gurton's Needle." It may occasion surprise that
such a play should have been the composition
of a scholar, and furnished enjoyment to
other scholars, who themselves represented
it. But the cause for surprise is rather that
Udall's comedy should have been produced
at a time when all classes relished and demanded just such coarseness and obscenity
as we find in " Gammer Gurton's Needle."

John Still [b. 1543—d. 1607-8], the author
of the second earliest comedy in our language, son of William Still, Esq., of Grant-
ham, in Lincolnshire, graduated at Christ

College, Cambridge, and entering the church was rapidly preferred, finally becoming Bishop of Bath and Wells. At the age of twenty-three Still wrote the play which commends him to our notice. It is to be observed that in later life, when Vice-Chancellor of Cambridge, he was called upon to oppose the performance of an English play before Queen Elizabeth at the University as unbefitting its learning and dignity.

There were many reasons why Comedy should precede Tragedy in dramatic evolution. The fun-making scenes in the Moralities were, in reality, foreign matter, and could be detached and acted alone. Comedy appeals to a wider audience. Latin models can be easily followed. Not so difficult of invention as Tragedy, as it requires less imagination and deals with more familiar objects ; a certain love of jesting and buffoonery innate in the English race. All these reasons conspired to produce our early Comedy before Tragedy, and some of these influences are visible later in the Romantic drama, and even in our plays of to-day.

The solemnity of the liturgy was replaced in the Mysteries and Miracles by a feeling of serious sacredness. This in its turn was

supplanted by a serious moral feeling in the
Moralities. This recognition of the sober
side and responsibilities of life has always
permeated the drama. From the first it is
seen to be an essential part of a play's existence. As this serious element is found in a
greater or less degree, so do we find the
varieties of the drama from the Tragedy to
the Farce. In the latter it is barely noticeable ; in the former it absorbs everything
else. From the Mysteries, Miracles and
Moralities then, aided by the Chronicle Histories, Seneca and his Italian imitators, was
Tragedy derived.

The history of this phase of our drama is
interwoven with that of an attempt to enforce
the rules of classical composition on the
dramatists of England. When the attention
of learned and cultured men was attracted
by the stage, they endeavored to impose upon
it the regulations then accepted throughout
Europe and particularly in Italy, as indicative
of good taste and style. At that time, the
sixteenth century, the Renaissance, that had
begun in Italy two centuries before, and had
enthroned that country as the intellectual
leader and superior, was making its influence
felt in England. There was soon a group of

English classical scholars as brilliant as any in Europe. These scholars were profoundly impressed and influenced by their Italian models, and though the independent English spirit became more and more manifest, they have never entirely shaken off this influence. Nor would that be desirable. Surrey and Wyatt introduced the sonnet and blank verse from Italy. Spencer's "Fairy Queen" was modeled after the Italian romantic epics. Translations of Italian novels flooded the book-stalls, and to these do we owe some of our most charming and valuable plays of Shakespeare and others. It is only natural that the Latin and Italian dramas should be imitated by scholars. Seneca, a faulty imitator of the Greek, was chosen as the model playwright. In his plays he has replaced action by rhetoric and at once perverted and lowered the standard of the Greek drama, which he imitated. Therefore, as a guide upon whose works others should plan theirs, he is pernicious and pseudo-classic. Not perceiving this fact, his plays were translated and his rules faithfully followed by learned men, such as Fulke Greville, Lord Brooke, George Gascoigne and Samuel Daniel, who endeavored to give a tendency to the English drama at once false and foreign. These efforts had no effect upon its development, however, and are only interesting as showing the continuous revolt against the Romantic or native English drama. The Latin trage- dies, such as George Buchanan's " Jeptha " and John Rightwise's " Dido," written for and performed in the Universities, were unqualified failures. These men, who under- took to set a pattern of what they thought was a purer style, did not see the mistake they were making, nor, fortunately, were they able to cope with the innate good taste of the people. The Romantic School of dramatists, who represented the popular taste and demands, felt that it was action, not didactic rhetoric and eloquence, that composed the essence of the drama. That there must be life, vigor, variety, conflicts of persons, pas- sions and events, and a final climax or catas- trophe, all depicted, not merely described.

" Gorboduc," the first tragedy written in English, though patterned after Seneca, is founded on a popular fable, showing thereby the irresistible native spirit. It is praised very highly by Sidney in his " Defence of Poesy." " It is full," he says, " of stately speeches and well-sounding phrases, climbing

to the height of Seneca his style." The
only grave fault he finds is non-observance of
the unity of time. So were the greatest literary men of the period completely misled by
false classical ideas. "Gorboduc" is composed of dissertations and monologues. All
the action occurs behind the scenes, and is
merely reported by messengers and com-
mented upon on the stage itself. The language is not natural and spontaneous. Each
person delivers a set oration and then steps
aside for the next to do likewise. The
speeches of the individual characters average
some fifty lines. Each act is concluded with
a chorus spoken by "four ancient and sage
men of Britain," which contains some of the
best poetry of the play Though any amount
of blood is shed, not a drop flows on the
stage. Dumb shows were given before each
act to reveal in metaphorical pantomime the
meaning of what followed. These pageants
served the double purpose of elucidating the
play and relieving the dull solemnity of the
performance. The play is the story of Gorboduc, King of Britain, dividing his kingdom
during his lifetime between his sons Ferrex
and Porrux. The inevitable results follow ;
envy, ingratitude, hatred, murder, civil con-

flict ; Gorboduc, his queen and both sons, all fall victims to his mistaken policy, and are slain. The chief defect in the story of the play is prolonging it after the death of all the principal personages, when a new set of motives of necessity arise. It is the first play written in blank verse.

Norton, a learned lawyer, and Sackville, a learned courtier, were the authors of "Gorboduc." The first mentioned, a strict reformer of the bitterest sect, was by four years his collaborator's senior. Sackville, in early life wild and extravagant, afterwards reformed. He had a great part in the compilation of the poems known as "The Mirror for Magistrates," which connect the works of Lydgate and Spencer. "Gorboduc," the work of these two men, was first performed at Whitehall, before the Queen, in 1561.

The second tragedy of the English stage is "The Misfortunes of Arthur." Thomas Hughes was the author. Francis Bacon, Christopher Yelveston and John Lancaster, gentlemen of Gray's Inne, devised the Dumb-shows. Like "Gorboduc," it was written by learned men. The play is a decided improvement upon its predecessor in dramatic painting, language and spon-

taneity. The story is, however, indescrib-
ably loathsome. In this tragedy a character
is imported from Seneca destined to great
popularity and long life through the works
of Brooke, Kyd, Jonson, Shakespeare, etc.,
viz. : The Ghost.

The pseudo-classic school was not without
its beneficial influence on the English drama.
It brought about a respect for studied
thought as well as the mere dramatizations
of a story, and compelled play-wrights to consider whether mature reflection and dramatic
action might not be harmonized. Finally it
introduced blank verse, imperfect to be sure,
but still blank verse. "Gorboduc" was
printed at least twenty years before the production of Marlowe's "Tamburlaine."

Worthy of special mention is Richard
Edward's "Damon and Pithias," played possibly in 1564-5, and printed in 1571, and Robert
Wilmot's "Tancred and Gismunda" (originally acted in 1568, published in 1592). The
former is Edwards' only extant play, and was
a most popular one. This success was partly
owing to the commendation of the Queen,
partly to the novelty of bringing stories from
profane history upon the stage. There is no
division into acts in the play, but the dialogue,

covering a period of two months, continues
to the end.   The story is, with slight varia-
tions, the familiar one.   The play teems with
proverbs. " Tancred and Gismunda " was the
production of five gentlemen, but was afterwards so much altered by one of them, Robert
Wilmot, that he is usually named as the author.
King Tancred, actuated by excessive paternal
love, refuses his daughter Gismunda permis-
sion to marry a second time.   She becomes a
victim of her passion. Tancred discovers her
lover, causes him to be slain, and his heart sent
in a golden goblet to Gismunda.   She takes
poison, and dying begs to be buried with her
lover.   Tancred, overcome with remorse and
sorrow, slays himself.   There is lacking action
and skill in construction in the piece, but the
thought and language is often beautiful, as
when Tancred addresses the dead body of his
daughter :

" Oh, fair in life ! thrice fairer in thy death !
   Dear to thy father in thy life thou wert ;
   But in thy death, dearest unto his heart ;
   I kiss thy paled cheeks, and close thine eyes.
   This duty once I promised to myself
   Thou shouldst perform to me ; but, ah ! false
        hope,
   Now ruthful, wretched king, what resteth thee ?

From the "Minutes of the Revels," between 1568 and 1580, Mr. Collier has obtained a list of fifty-two plays. None of these remain. Even their authors are unknown. Written at a time when only wealthy scholars could have their plays published, and who did not always do so, and when also a successful piece was carefully kept from the printer, that it might be played only by the rightful owners, they were eventually forgotten and perished. A brilliant success, like "Gorboduc," was pirated and thus preserved. A few were in this manner rescued. Of those that perished we can safely say that they were intended merely for popular amusement, and that it was the people who supported them.

The play-wright began to derive material from the love stories of history and mythology, and a style of play grew up full of absurdities and extravagances, careless of rules, but having a variety and vigor that took strong hold on popular favor. In spite of scholarly and pedantic hostility this "people's drama" was encouraged by court as well as populace, and continued to thrive and grow strong. In direct opposition to the pseudo-classic type, which it was to vanquish, yet it was to be greatly improved and modi-

fied by that type. Learned dramatists were
won to the side of the Romantic drama and
became its earnest supporters. Edwards and
Wilmot were both scholars. It is to this period
that "Damon and Pithias," "Tancred and
Gismunda," the earliest "Romeo and Juliet,"
and Whetstone's "Promos and Cassandra,"
belong. But we cannot judge of the merit
and value of the drama of that time by the
few plays remaining to us ; it is rather by the
contemporary and often hostile criticism, of
which there is considerable, that it is valuable.
Sidney complained of the lack of art. North-
brooke of the immorality connected with the
stage. Stephen Gosson, a former dramatist
and actor, attacked both professions fiercely.
This brought out many replies. Thomas
Lodge, in "Plays Confuted in Five Actions,"
shows that the play-wrights drew their plots
from Italian translations, mythology, classical
history, Latin plays, and the romances of the
middle ages. Whetstone attacked the romantic plays because of their impossibilities. He
says, "Then in three hours runs he through
the world ; marries, gets children ; makes
children men, men to conquer kingdoms,
murder monsters, and bringeth gods from
heaven, and fetcheth devils from hell." Sid·

ney complains, "For where the stage should always represent but one place, and the uttermost time presupposed in it should be, both by Aristotle's precept and common reason, but one day, there is both many days and many places inartificially imagined. . . . Many things may be told which can not be shown."

These critics desired to separate distinctly Tragedy and Comedy ; to permit no intermingling ; to preserve the classical unities of time, place and action ; to describe rather than depict action. Upheld by the French Academy, these principles produced the artificial and unnatural drama of Racine, Corneille, etc., and it was not until the daring master-genius of Victor Hugo had produced his " Hernani," that they were overthrown and their bad effect recognized in that country. In England our Romantic drama refused to obey a single one of these rules. There was nothing in the shape of a story that it would not utilize ; hence it has been defined as " a represented story."

In 1512–13 Henry VIII. introduced into England a species of the drama long popular on the continent, but until then unseen in Britain, the Masque. In order to treat of this type in full we shall have to deviate for a short time from the course of our subject proper, and even to pass into the regions of later work, disregarding chronology.

The Masque is a dramatic species midway between a pageant and a play ; a spectacle, consisting of a combination of dancing and music with poetry and declamation, whose chief characteristic is magnificence of production. It makes but little demand for acting, yet a great deal for splendor and beauty. The mechanic and author share the honors. The actors are insignificant. Complicated machines, elaborate scenic effects, music and dancing are the necessities.

With the very rich the Masque became a favorite amusement. It was a gorgeous parade of their wealth and power ; a display to produce which a whole army of mechanics and performers were necessary. At one Masque given in Italy one hundred and sixty actors took part. The principal actors represented Olympian Deities and personifications of the Virtues. The Masques given before Lucrezia Borgia (1502) and Leonora of Aragon (1474) were of a consecutive nature ; that is, consisted of a series of shows rather than one. In 1513, however, at Urbino, this processional idea was made prominent and cars were introduced. A Carnival at Venice is simply a phase of the Masque. A Veiled Prophet's Procession, or Mardi Gras, is what is left to us of this type. Essentially an Italian production, it lost much in transplanting to English soil. The artistic nature of the people was not highly cultured. They were defective in the fine arts, such as music, architecture and painting. These hardy, storm-beaten, warlike islanders had not the leisure nor the surroundings to call forth the obscure want of these things. Yet the English were not insensible to their beauty, only incapable of producing them in their highest form. Therefore foreign artists were imported, necessarily of a second rank, else they would have remained at home. Nor was Elizabeth, in whose reign they became popular, willing to expend lavishly her wealth in the manner requisite for a Masque as produced in Italy; although she was greatly pleased when her nobles did so in her honor, as did Leicester at Kenilworth. It was not until the Stuarts reigned that this form of entertainment reached its highest development in England. James and Charles were extremely fond of the Masque, and during their rule their court rivaled that of the Italians in the magnificence of this dramatic type, and far excelled it in poetical worth. To English dramatists alone belongs the honor of elevating the Masque to the plane of literature. From the pens of Jonson, Beaumont, Fletcher, and Milton, came Masques of literary merit and powers to please in reading as well as representation. Jonson and Inigo Jones, the architect, fixed the type for English writers to follow. Some of these Masques cost £3,000 to produce. On " The Triumph of Peace," designed by Shirley and Inigo Jones, and presented in 1634 at Whitehall, £2,000 was expended. Often royal and noble personages took part in these performances, as in some of Jonson's pieces we find that the Queen and her ladies assumed the characters. An Anti-Masque was often introduced to lighten the entertainment with fun. Deprived of their scenic and other accompaniments, the Masques call for great flights of the imagination. Nevertheless, so much learning and genius was expended upon them, so many beauties are to be found in them, that they can still be read with pleasure. Jonson is at his best in his Masques.

Like every other prominent feature of the national life, the Masque was in time incorporated in the drama. We find it in Shakespeare's " Tempest," and in Fletcher's " Maid's Tragedy." A Mask of Madmen is introduced by Webster in his tragedy, " The Duchess." To be given on the stage the Masque had to be much simplified and quickly disposed of. Often it was inappropriately utilized, probably because of its powerful effect on the people's imagination. The last and most brilliant literary achievement in this dramatic field was Milton's " Comus." It is in composition and intrinsic merit far superior to everything else of its kind, having nothing in common with those entertainments whose chief interest centered in glittering and magnificent surroundings. But the Masque has disappeared, or rather degenerated, into pantomimic processions. Designed for a lower order of intellect, as the race progressed, it resigned all literary and dramatic claims, and became simply a vulgar show or parade.

We have spoken of the Hybrid Plays, touched upon the Interlude, and deviated somewhat to view the Masques, now we must return to Comedy and Tragedy. The earliest Tragedies were founded on the legendary history of England, as "Gorboduc," "The Misfortunes of Arthur," "Locrine," and "King Lear." The first two we have already mentioned. The stories of all are well known. From dealing with legendary characters it was but a step to treating historical ones. And it is worthy of remark that in English literature alone did this treatment attain something approaching perfection. In other languages the attempts made to dramatize their national history do not deserve the name of Chronicle Plays. A Chronicle Play should treat in a single action of the leading events of a reign, not be a selected and dramatized national episode. Our Chronicle Plays, having for their object the representation of the national annals, cover nearly the whole field of English history.

Bale's "King John," which we have already mentioned, heads the list of Historical or Chronicle Plays. "The Troublesome Reign of King John," "The True Tragedy of Richard III.," "Richard Tertius," "The Famous Victories of Henry V.," "The Contention of the Two Famous Houses of York," all belong to this early and defective period. Though often interesting and vigorous, they are crude and rough. "Richard Tertius" is a Latin Chronicle Play, by Dr. Legge. " Edward III." is of a higher order than any of the preceding, and has been ascribed to Shakespeare, but without sufficient authority to be accepted as his.   Marlowe's " Edward II." was the first really excellent Chronicle. Not printed until 1598, it was, however, probably written in 1590.   Then follow Peele's " Edward I.," in 1593.   Thomas Heywood's two parts of " Edward IV." (in which the story of Jane Shore forms a principal element).   "If You Know Not Me, You Know Nobody " (a play upon the reign of Mary, and the accession of Elizabeth).   Rowley's "When You See Me, You Know Me " (the reign of Henry VIII.).

The Chronicle plays are very unequal in merit.   In Shakespeare and Marlowe they reach their highest perfection, and in Rowley the lowest.   Together with Shakespeare's and subsequent Chronicles there is an almost continuous series of studies in English history from 1119 to 1588, from the accession of John to the defeat of the Armada—nearly four centuries.   These plays served a noble purpose in educating and enlightening the people concerning their country's history.   In " The Apology for Actors," Heywood pointed out how useful these plays were in instructing the ignorant, and reminding the learned of the great facts of history and morals.

Closely allied to the Historical or Chronicle plays are those that are biographical, such as have for their subjects popular heroes, whether real or mythical. The earliest to be acted was "Sir Thomas More." Then followed "The Life and Death of Thomas, Lord Cromwell," "Sir John Oldcastle," "Sir Thomas Wyatt," "Perkin Warbeck," "The Fair Maid of the West," "Capt. Thomas Stukeley," "Pinner of Wakefield," etc. Some of these are by unknown authors, two have been wrongly attributed to Shakespeare. While of inferior workmanship, yet all breathing the independent, adventure-loving English spirit, they were based some on real some on mythical personages, and dealt partly in facts and largely in legends. Three plays of this class celebrated that popular highwayman, Robin Hood. In all is the attempt made to depict the English gentleman, bold, honorable and adventurous. It is the nation's spirit working to the surface.

From the biographical to the domestic drama it was but a step. From treating of the principal events in the lives of popular heroes, to treating stirring events in contemporaneous society was the natural development of play-writing. That the contemporary events chosen should have been those of a morbid and fascinating interest, as some famous crime, is not to be wondered at, but expected. Horrible stories of passion and murder, found in Holinshed's and Stow's Chronicles, were used as subjects for gloomy, realistic plays, in which the minutest details were adhered to and all ornament or invention excluded. These plays are bold studies of real life, where all romance and glamour is dispensed with, and where licentiousness, brutality, murder and avarice are pictured as they are. Yet this type seems to have been very popular, despite its brutal nature.

The five tragedies representative of this class given by Symonds are : "Warning for Fair Women" (1599), "A Yorkshire Tragedy" (1608), "Arden of Feversham" (1592), "Woman Killed with Kindness" (1603), and the "Witch of Edmonton" (1623). These extend into a later period than I wish to treat of here, which fact shows how difficult it is in literature as in history to mark off divisions and how inevitably these divisions will overlap one another.

" Arden of Feversham " was based on " The lamentable and true tragedy of Master Arden of Feversham, in Kent, who was most wickedly murdered by the means of his disloyal and wanton wife, who, for the love she bore to one Mosbie, hired two desperate ruffians, Black Will and Shagbag, to kill him." This play, and " The Yorkshire Tragedy," have been assigned to Shakespeare, but while authorities differ, it is safe to say the weight of evidence is against this theory of their authorship.

There is a purer and higher tone in " A Woman Killed with Kindness," than is usually found in the domestic type. Here is a realism that elevates, a vileness that displays purity, and a virtuous character revealed by others' wickedness. The picturing of character and passion is the great object in this as in other plays of its kind. Particularly is this so in the " Witch of Edmonton," the title role of which has no superior of its type in English literature. Little claim is made by these plays to artistic value, although there is often a vein of excellent poetry.

We have now reached that point in the history of our drama, where the expression of a type or species of play was found in some particular writer. Where the spirit of the time is best studied and more clearly revealed in the works of some one genius, than it would be in all the contemporaneous literature. We have reached the period of activity of Shakespeare's immediate predecessors : Kyd, Lyly, Greene, Peele, Nash, Lodge and Marlowe.

Thomas Kyd, the circumstances of whose life and death are unknown, was the founder of the " Tragedy of Blood." The characters of this species are the noble and fearless lover, the beautiful and oppressed heroine, the generous old man, the consummate villain, the villain's tools, paid assassins and a ghost. The peculiarites are intolerable wrongs, unmerited sufferings, secret malice. There are portraits of wildest insanity, extravagant love-making, fierce encounters. Kings, clowns, assassins, princes, ladies, fill the scene. Blood flows freely, and death reigns supreme. In the " Spanish Tragedy," that much ridiculed play, there are five murders, two suicides, two judicial executions, and one death in a duel. The principal character, Hieronymo, bites out his tongue, throws it down, kills his foe and then himself. Such is an example of the frightful scenes our ancestors called Tragedy. The people of that day were pleased with blood

and had nerves of iron. Their sympathies
were only reached by uppiling horrible events.
Every imaginable means was resorted to to
stir their sluggish blood and thrill them.
These tragedies have aptly been compared
to a fierce tempest in which everything is
destroyed, and peace is only reached by annihilation.

JOHN LYLY, M. A., member of Magdalene
College, who had won fame by his "Euphues"
in 1579, attached himself to the Court in 1580,
and became a dramatist. He always desired
the office of Master of the Revels, but never
obtained it. For this purpose he turned his
attention to writing plays which have been
styled Court Comedies. These plays formed
a new species of drama, a species which was to
affect all succeeding dramatic literature. This
type of comedy, which Lyly invented, and
which gives him an important place as a
dramatist, was extremely popular for some
twenty years. The distinguishing marks
of this "Court" or "Euphuistic" Comedy
are extravagant language, studied manner-
isms, abundant antitheses, fanciful conceits,
superficial allegory and repartee. Added
to these Lyly first introduced witty prose
dialogue and the custom of disguising female

character in male attire in the drama. So
that while there is much to condemn and
lament, yet there is something to praise in
Lyly. Nor must Lyly be blamed severely
for adopting and nourishing this comedy of
affectation for he simply expressed a phase of
English literary life that existed in his time.
It was a piece of road over which the literature had naturally to pass. To the people of
that period, ignorant of science, allegory and
symbolism deeply appealed. The scholars in
their study of the ancients had not yet learned
to distinguish between the good and the bad
authors, but accepted them all. Hence in the
writings of the day, as in their conversation,
there is found a sacrificing of purity, form
and truth, to a straining after effect, a tendency to allegory, and an abuse of classical
learning. Lyly was without doubt original
in his works. Nothing like his comedies had
ever before been seen in England. They are
wanting in plot, action and intrigue, are
merely a succession of brilliant scenes, where
the language is sparkling and the allegory
interesting. Of his eight comedies six were
given before Elizabeth, and all are full of
extravagant and judicious praise of the
Queen. In "Endimion" Elizabeth is thinly

disguised as " Cynthia," in " Sapho and Phao " by " Sapho " and so on. Platonic love, roman- tic devotion, the nobleness of a ruler prefer- ring the toils of sovereignty to the pleasures of love, England's enemies, defeated and dis- appointed, actuate and permeate all his works. The term " Euphuism," which has been applied to this style of writing, is taken from the name of Lyly's novel, " Euphues," in which he first popularized and propagated this kind of prose literature. His lyrics, with which his plays are adorned, should be men- tioned for their rare beauty. Lyly's comedies, though little noted to-day, mark an epoch and distinguish him as a discoverer.

GREENE, PEELE, NASH and LODGE form a quartette of poets of peculiar interest from their associations in life, work and death. They were all well born and well educated ; all came from the universities and with the degree of Master of Arts. Despite their birth and attainments they were excluded from respectable society because of their loose lives and profanity. Three of these men after leading wretched, licentious lives died mis- erably, barely reckoning forty years each. Lodge alone extricated himself from this wild life, became respectable, and reached a good old age, dying, as we are told, "decently of the plague," in 1625.

The best known and most erratic genius of this quartette, ROBERT GREENE, was a man of brilliant powers, and low passions, doomed to the bitter disappointment of being far excelled in his profession, and to the just punishment of a miserable end to a miserable life. When Greene first engaged in play-writing, rimed dramas were very popular, and in this style of writing he soon took a first place. He bitterly opposed the introduction of blank verse, which Marlowe made in "Tamburlaine," and which revolutionized the stage. He quarrelled with both Marlowe and Nash on this subject, but being unable to oppose the popular demands, was compelled to dispense with the old method and adopt the new. In doing this, he lost his pre-eminence, and was forced into the subordinate position of an imitator. But no sooner had Greene yielded to Marlowe's ascendancy, than he was called upon to submit to a still greater conqueror, Shakespeare. He could not retreat twice gracefully, especially since the second genius was neither a learned nor a travelled gentleman.

Greene could not forgive the dramatist who by industry and sobriety was winning fame

and wealth, while he was ending an ill-spent
life in wretched poverty. In his time he had
been a popular author, but working not for
posterity but for ephemeral fame and money,
he received only that for which he had bar-
gained. On his death-bed he bitterly and
inexcusably attacked the stage, the actors,
and Shakespeare. Since the first had given
him his living, the second had once reckoned
him in their ranks, and the third only surpassed him by reason of superior excellence
he should not have complained. It was the
old story of blaming art and artists for the
results of individual sin. Greene's novels
form the better part of his works. His plays
lack unity of plot and character portraitures.
There is shown an excellent story-telling faculty and the power to employ at once a variety of motives and a simplicity of detail.
The main defects are an inappropriate use of
Latin mythology and a failure to appreciate
the dignity of the drama. None of Greene's
earlier works are extant. Of his later plays
the most celebrated are " Looking-Glass for
London " (a joint work with Lodge), " Al-
phonso, Prince of Aragon " and " James The
Fourth of Scotland." The last is probably
his best.

GEORGE PEELE was not a prolific writer, nor did he have a pronounced effect on the literature of his time. While he was not an original thinker, yet he took high rank as a poet. His descriptions are graceful, his verse is sweet, and his feeling is natural and tender. He might have been a greater man had not the necessities of his time drawn him into an extravagance and exaggeration foreign to him. Even as it is, his writing shows unusual dignity and repose. His best works are: " The Arraignment of Paris " and " David and Bethsaba." The former is a classical Masque and the latter a modern Mystery Play. " The Old Wives' Tales " is claimed by some to be the source of Milton's " Comus." His other dramatic productions do not call for more special mention than to say that they are dull, insipid and extravagant.

THOMAS NASH was the bitterest satirist of his own, if not of any age, of English literature. He avoided learned displays of rhetoric. drew bold caricatures, stinging epigrams and invectives. His method of arguing by abuse and ridicule made him the first pamphleteer, if not the first dramatist of that time. " Ingenious, fluent, facetious Thomas Nash," says Dekker, "from what abundant

pen flowed honey to thy friends and mortal
aconite to thy enemies." Nash is supposed
to have been a collaborator in Marlowe's
"Queen Dido." "Will Summer's Testament," is his best known play. Nash is particularly remembered for his staunch defense
of his dead friend Greene's reputation against
the attacks of Gabriel Harvey.

THOMAS LODGE, son of a Lord Mayor, was
successively scholar, actor, poet, adventurer
and physician. In comparison to his other
writings his plays are insignificant. He
collaborated with Greene in the composition of "Looking-Glass of London," and
produced the stiff, unnatural tragedy of " The
Wounds of Civil War." Lodge's claims as a
poet must rest upon his lyrics.

CHRISTOPHER MARLOWE was born at Canterbury in the same year with Shakespeare,
1564. Although a shoemaker's son, he was
given the advantages of a Cambridge education, probably by the assistance of some
wealthy gentleman, it is thought Sir Roger
Marwood. Of Marlowe it can be truly said
that he was born a poet. His first extant
work, a tragedy, showing the master of a new
style destined to revolutionize play-writing
and become the most perfect and attractive

type of the drama yet attained, was written at the age of twenty-two.

"Tamburlaine" made Marlowe at once famous and idolized. The rest of his life, but six years, he spent writing plays, a profession then tolerably remunerative. During this time he composed the second part of "Tamburlaine," "Dr. Faustus," "The Massacre at Paris," "The Jew of Malta," and "Edward II.," besides some exquisite poems and a part of the tragedy of "Dido." All of these plays in style, vigor and imagination far surpass everything that had preceded them.

When we look upon the crude compositions of the men who wrote before "Tamburlaine" appeared, and then upon the plays written after its production, we will not dispute Marlowe's claim to the title given him by his admirers of Father of English Dramatic Poetry.

Before Marlowe's time, although all kinds of plays had been attempted, none had been brought to any degree of perfection. Indeed, for this very lack of anything approaching perfection, the stamp of which genius alone can give, the stage was threatened with ruin. Abandoned by the scholars who desired an imitative art, debased by the multitude that wished only buffoonery and unnatural melodrama, derided by the Puritans and moralists who would have no plays at all, the drama trembled on the brink of ruin. From this impending danger it was Marlowe that rescued it, and thereby rendered an inestimable service to English literature. Marlowe's plays revived and purified dramatic taste, and gave fresh impetus to dramatic production.

Like all great workers, Marlowe made use of the best of all materials that were within his reach. He selected the popular Romantic drama, perceiving its eminent capabilities, as the type best suited for his purpose. He rejected the much-admired rime and adopted blank verse, for he beheld in it the highest form of poetry. To do this required confident courage, for before he wrote, blank verse, though used, had been lifeless. To inspire this verse with melody and meaning, and to unite it with the previously hostile element, the Romantic drama, in a manner at once elevating and successful, was the effort of a great genius. From a chaos he brought forth a drama. Nor was he ignorant of the service he rendered the stage. In his

prologue to " Tamburlaine" he openly proclaimed his purpose to win the populace.

> " From jigging veins of rhyming mother wits,
>   And such conceits as clownage keeps in pay."

This he succeeded in doing, so much so that
the English drama never returned to rime
except in a phase of its history which is to
be regarded merely as a conscious aberration
from its national course and from which it
soon returned.

Marlowe was one of the few men who
undertook to reform and elevate the stage,
and who succeeded. His services are twofold, *i. e.*, the introduction of a living blank
verse and the recognition and uniting of
proper dramatic materials. Yet we must
not believe or expect that Marlowe's poetry,
except in isolated passages, is comparable to
that of Shakespeare or Milton. It is merely
the intervening step between crudeness and
perfection. Marlowe is the pioneer that
clears the way for his greater successors.
His works are as a rule monotonous and
grandiloquent, though his poetry is at times
so beautiful " that it seems often the result of
momentary inspiration rather than the
studied style of a deliberate artist." He

seems incapable of sustained eloquence. Yet
in a different line, in an attempt of epical and
erotic poetry, as in "Hero and Leander," he
surpasses even the "Venus and Adonis" of
Shakespeare in excellence.

We have not yet spoken of Marlowe's life,
nor will we do more than barely touch on it.
He was notorious for license of speech and
looseness of habits; but, says Ward, indeed
truly, "For us, who can not penetrate through
the foul mists which obscured the career of
this fiery genius, it remains only to lament
the loss to our literature of the fruits of a
promise without parallel among our earlier—
indeed, with one exception, among all our
Elizabethan dramatists." Considering the
facts of Marlowe's dissipated life and early
death, he was only twenty-nine when murdered in a drunken brawl, that at the age of
twenty-two he produced a play that revolutionized the stage, the eminent value of the
plays written during his short career, and the
great services he rendered the English drama,
he is to be rated as one of the most original,
creative poets of the world.

Of the seven dramatists, upon whose lives
and works we have touched, Lyly represents
a peculiar and original style which has affected

in some degree all succeeding literature. Kyd stands for us as the representative of the Tragedy of Blood. Greene marks the advent of the Romantic play. Nash the introduction into prose of controversy and satire. Peele is an artistic poet not influencing but merely complying with the demands of his age. Lodge asserts the rare beauties of the lyric. It was left for Marlowe, the last and greatest of the seven, to select and combine the beauties of all the others with the faults of some of them, to prepare the way for the master mind that was to follow or as our Anglo-Saxon ancestors would have said, " The light that was to shine over many lands."

III.

SHAKESPEARE.

For the proper understanding and appreciation of a great man I believe it is a generally accepted theory that we must be familiar with the times in which he lived, the circumstances of his life, the people by whom he was surrounded, the materials at his disposal. Then in the study of a great dramatist we must consider not only the immediate products of his pen, but also the causes which called forth and the conditions which modified or affected in any vital manner his compositions. Foremost amongst this seemingly extraneous matter is the theatre. Without a certain knowledge of the stage and audience for which Shakespeare wrote we can not be said to have a thorough knowledge of Shakespeare himself. Much that is otherwise inexplicable or at least apparently superfluous reveals at once its significance and importance. Therefore I shall not hesitate to preface my remarks on Shakespeare by a cursory examination of the theatre.

In the beginning, as we have seen, the drama had no permanent home. There were no buildings set aside for such a purpose. The Mysteries were exhibited in churches or on movable platforms in the streets. The Moralities and Interludes were given in corporation halls, great lord's castles, or at inn yards. The first plays, such as " Gammer Gurton's Needle," were produced in the universities.

As priests at first, and later tradesmen and scholars, presented these plays, it is readily seen that if there was at this period no regular theatre, neither was there any regular, that is, professional acting. For a long time the ideas of acting and breadwinning were not connected. However, they began to be associated with the advent of the Interlude, and with the decline of the clown and the minstrel. Companies of actors sprang into existence. Some were attached to great households, others roved from place to place. The custom of a powerful baron maintaining such a company, which called itself his servants, became very popular. Even the Court kept its actors, and Mary is said to have spent large sums on their maintenance.

In an age without newspapers, next to
the pulpit, the stage, however rude, was
the most popular and influential educator
and guide. On account of this the actors
were at times licensed, at times restricted, at times prohibited in their performances. But despite all interferences and per-
secutions, supported by the people, the nobility and the Court, the stage thrived.
When prohibitory proclamations were issued
the representations did not cease, they simply
became clandestine.

Recognizing the fact that the English
drama was an outgrowth of the English
nature, and that all proclamations and laws
issued against it would be ineffectual to
suppress it, Elizabeth and her counselors
merely attempted to regulate the stage and
restrain it from excesses. Companies had
to be licensed or attached to some great
nobleman. Subjects pertaining to religion
or politics were rigorously prohibited.
During the time of Common Prayer and the
Plague plays were forbidden. Unless these
conditions were complied with actors were
considered as vagrants.

In spite of the active opposition of a certain
class, under the patronage of the Court, the

stage obtained a permanent footing in London. A Royal Grant was conferred upon the Earl of Leicester's players, who were headed by James Burbage, father of the celebrated Shakespearean actor, Richard Burbage.

Hostility was soon rife between the stage and its mother, the church. On the score of ungodliness theatrical performances were excluded from the city by the Common Council. Open warfare was at once declared between Court and city. The Privy Council commanded the Lord Mayor that he should permit six companies to play in London, " By reason that they are appointed to play this Christmas before her Majesty." Finally, under the powerful protection of the Queen, the players were installed in permanent buildings in the suburbs of London, in Shoreditch, at Blackfriars, and on Bankside.

Previous to this plays had been commonly acted on scaffolds, erected in the yards and galleries of inns. And it was the scandals, caused chiefly by the surroundings, that attended these open-air performances which the city had been attacking.

In 1576 the Lord Mayor gave, unwillingly, a tacit consent to the erection of the first theatre in England. From this year may be said to date the modern English drama, for in this year the drama ceased to be nomadic. The first building put up for theatrical purposes was in Shoreditch, and was appropriately styled, the Theatre. Shortly afterwards a second arose near by, which took its name from the plot of ground on which it stood, and was called, the Curtain. In the same year arose the Blackfriar's, named from its situation. This was occupied by Lord Leicester's players. These theatres were crude, wooden structures.

In 1593, the most famous theatre in the history of the stage, as being the scene of Shakespeare's exploits, the Globe, was erected on the Bankside by Richard Burbage, leader of the Lord Chamberlaine's Men. It was constructed of wood ; hexagon-shaped without and round within. There were two doors, one leading into the body of the house, the other to the actors' dressing-room.

Excepting a thatched roof, or " heaven," projecting over the stage, the building was open to the sky. Railed off from the stage was a large central place where the audience stood. Around this central place were private boxes for those who could pay for them.

The Globe was burned in 1613 during a performance, probably, of Shakespeare's " Henry
VIII.," and in the following year was rebuilt,
this time with a tiled roof. Burbage's company played here in the summer, and at the
Blackfriar's in the winter.

Another famous theatre was the Fortune,
which was the most commodious and elegant
of any that had then been built in England.
In 1623 it was rebuilt—it is thought of brick.

The opposition to the stage manifested by
certain classes, and which resulted in the
censorship of the Master of the Revels, a
still prevailing custom, had, nevertheless, a
beneficial effect. To it we may ascribe the
comparative purity of moral tone contrasted
with the contemporaneous drama of France
and Italy ; also its total lack of political and
religious satire. Moreover, the actor became
more respectable and wealthy, and altogether
the drama and its appurtenances made rapid
progress.

The theatres were either private or public.
The first were smaller in size, roofed over and
frequented by a more select audience. Blackfriar's was a private, the Globe and the Fortune public theatres. The performances were
given in the afternoon, beginning at three

o'clock and usually lasted about two hours.
This was in order to let the audience get
home before dark. When a play was going
to begin flags were hoisted and trumpets
blown. The piece of the day was generally
closed with an address to the sovereign. Then
followed a farce. Playbills were used to
announce the show ; those of tragedies being
in red letters. Entrance prices varied according to the theatre, location, etc. For ordinary shows three pennies were paid. There
was a two-penny gallery in the larger
theatres, which fee was probably additional
to the one for admission. On a good night
prices ranged from sixpence to half a crown.
The commonest part of the audience stood in
the open yard. In private theatres this yard
or pit was furnished with benches. Fashion-
ables sat on three-legged stools on the stage.
This was vigorously opposed in public
theatres, but the custom was not abandoned
until the time of David Garrick. Pick-
pockets and cut-purses were common, and are
repeatedly referred to in the earlier plays.
If one were caught he was tied to one of the
pillars on the stage and pelted and scoffed
during the performance. Attention was con-
centrated on the play and the actors. The

scenes and properties were left very largely to the imagination of the spectators. The stage was narrow, projecting into the yard and surrounded by the audience. There being no scenery, the poet had to fill out much with description. A raised platform at the back represented castle walls, balconies, etc. Painted boards announced the location of the scene. The wardrobe was rich and varied but not correct. Dramatists were often actors and managers, as Shakespeare, Jonson, Heywood, Marlowe, etc. Boys acted female characters. Actresses were seen but once on the stage until the Restoration, in 1668. The theatre libraries were very valuable and so carefully hoarded that we have received many plays only through pirates. Having handed a MSS. to a manager few play-wrights ever thought of publishing their work.

Such were the theatres and their surroundings in the Elizabethan age, the age which produced the greatest poet of English literature, and the giant intellect of all literature, Shakespeare. Baptized April 26th, 1564, his birthday being probably April 23d, William Shakespeare was the third child, and first son of John and Mary Shakespeare. His two elder sisters died in their infancy and before his birth. Afterwards were born several other children.

John Shakespeare was a glover and although unable to write, was highly respected and filled the offices of bailiff and alderman of Stratford. He afterwards became involved in pecuniary troubles and was deprived of his position. He is supposed to have been largely dependent upon his son Wiiliam in his later days.

The name ef Shakespeare occurs for some hundred years before our great dramatist appeared, but there is nothing in any way remarkable connected with it until then.

A grant of arms was made to John Shakespeare, William's father, but it is believed to have been due to the influence of his mother's family, the Ardens. This was ancient and considerable, deriving its name from the forest of Arden near which it had possessions and tracing its descent even into far Anglo-Saxon times.

About the life of William Shakespeare himself I quote Stevens' familiar summary. "All that is known with any degree of certainty concerning Shakespeare is that he was born at Stratford-upon-Avon, married and had

children there; went to London, where he
commenced actor and wrote poems and plays;
returned to Stratford made his will, died and
was buried."

And though this summary may be somewhat too brief, it is, nevertheless, representative to us of our limited acquaintance with the
actual facts of our great poet's life. Very nearly
everything else concerning Shakespeare with
which we are familiar, is merely anecdote.
The story of his beginning his theatrical
career by holding gentlemen's horses before
the door of the theatre, and that of the deer
stealing, as well as several less savory ones,
cannot be authenticated, and must be dis-
missed from all serious consideration. Attempts have been made to show that Shakespeare was a wool-stapler, a butcher, a
farmer, a school-teacher, a lawyer's apprentice, a surgeon's apprentice, and a soldier.
Also he has been proven (?) to have been
respectively a Protestant, an Atheist, and a
Catholic. On the questions of his religion,
and the manner in which his early youth was
passed, we must be content to remain in
ignorance.

It is common to regard Shakespeare as a
man of very little learning, and his works as

the productions of a wild, irresistible genius. This idea is based partly on Jonson's well-known remark of Shakespeare knowing " little Latin and less Greek ; " partly to the mistaken opinions so boldly asserted by the commentators of succeeding ages, who were so little able to understand his genius and who so servilely followed the French school. But the truth seems to be that Shakespeare was a well educated man. The very fact of his knowledge of Greek and Latin, though imperfect, goes to prove that he was not the illiterate savage he was long considered. Besides there are few men long out of the walls of their schools who retain much more than a slight remembrance of the classical languages. Also his acquaintance with French and Italian is undisputed, and it is probable that he may not have been wholly ignorant of Spanish. Add to this a wide and varied knowledge of men and their callings, of the phenomena of nature, mythology, and history, and recalling his remarkable vocabulary, a proof of his extensive reading, and no sane man can longer refuse to Shakespeare the claim of having been well educated. Unless, indeed, we are to measure a man's learning by the number of years spent within the walls of a school and the degrees conferred upon him by the universities.

Certain it is that Shakespeare was married before he was nineteen years old to Anne Hathaway, a woman some eight years his senior. Anne bore him three children : Susanna, Judith and Hamnet, the last two being twins. Hamnet died at the age of eleven. The last descendants of Susanna and Judith died before the close of the seventeenth century. So there survive no immediate representatives of the great poet. Late in 1586 Shakespeare left Stratford for London, whether on account of domestic infelicity, a deer-stealing expedition, or simply an attachment conceived for the stage, we are not able to say. Suffice it that he went to London, and in three years became a sharer in the Blackfriar's Theatre. Peele at this time was a member of the same company, the Lord Chamberlain's Players, and as he was then at the height of his fame and popularity as a dramatist, it is probable that Shakespeare's services were utilized as an actor rather than a play-wright. There is every reason to believe that he was a good actor. His instructions to the players in " Hamlet " alone stamp him as familiar with

the theory of his art. He is recorded as
playing the ghost in "Hamlet," and tradition
speaks of him as Adam in " As You Like It."
After Peele left the Lord Chamberlain's
Players, Shakespeare was called upon to show
his skill as a dramatist, and as his talent in
this line became apparent, he was left little
time for acting. The great popularity of his
plays, and his published poems "Venus and
Adonis " and "Lucrece," soon placed him in
the first rank of poets and dramatists. By
his talents, and from what we can learn, his
sobriety and industry, Shakespeare elevated
a despised calling, and acquired a considerable fortune. That he counted amongst his
friends and patrons such gentlemen as the
Earl of Southampton and Pembroke, is one
proof of the higher tone of his life when
compared with his contemporaries and predecessors. In time he was able to purchase
considerable property at Stratford, and retire
in plenty from the stage. The remainder of
his life was passed in producing the mature
works of his genius while living quietly with
his family at New Place in Stratford. "The
latter part of his life," says Rowe, "was
spent, as all men of good sense will wish
theirs may be, in ease, retirement and the

society of his friends." As to his personal attractions we are told that he was a handsome, agreeable and witty gentleman.

These are the main reliable facts in the life of .William Shakespeare ; actor, author, manager, gentleman. And from these we will learn that there is little to interfere with the noblest idea we can form of his character and conduct. The custom of attaching unsavory anecdotes to the name of a great man can not be sufficiently frowned upon. Man's life is filled with enough real mistakes and weaknesses, and there is no necessity to accept pure tradition in order to prove him human.

All attempts to classify Shakespeare's works must be largely arbitrary. If an exact chronological order is observed, there is no great degree of certainty to reward the student ; if the divisions of Comedy, History and Tragedy, there is much perplexity and doubt. Yet to treat our subject at all intelligently and systematically, it is necessary to adopt some scheme of classification. Contenting ourselves then with approximate dates, and dispensing with absolute correctness, we will take the year 1600 and arrange Shakespeare's plays in two classes, viz.: those that appeared before and those that appeared after the year 1600 ; that is, the earlier and the later plays.   These two classes we will subdivide into Comedies, Histories and Tragedies.

The tests which enable us to determine the approximate date of a play are twofold, the external and the internal.   The first consists of obtaining the latest date at which it must have been in existence, by means of mention in books and documents of a certain date. The latter, the internal, consists in allusions in the play itself ; in the style, versification and mental development.   What is meant by the mental development is the display of perception of character, depth, force, magnitude of idea, treatment of subject, etc.   As it would be folly to ascribe " Macbeth " to his youth or the "Comedy of Errors " to his maturity.   The very nature of the plays makes this evident to even a casual reader.

Keeping our landmark, the year 1600, plainly in view, we find that previous to that time, or in his earlier period, Shakespeare wrote nine comedies, nine histories and two tragedies.   In his later period we find five comedies, one history and eleven tragedies.

I. THE EARLIER PERIOD.

(a) *Comedies.*

Love's Labour's Lost.
Comedy of Errors.
Two Gentlemen of Verona.
Taming of the Shrew.
All's Well That Ends Well.
Merry Wives of Windsor.
Merchant of Venice.
A Midsummer Night's Dream.
Much Ado About Nothing.

(b) *Histories.*

King John.
Richard II.
Henry IV., 2 parts.
Henry V.
Henry VI., 3 parts.
Richard III.

(c) *Tragedies.*

Titus Andronicus.
Romeo and Juliet.

II. THE LATER PERIOD.

(a) *Comedies.*

Twelfth Night.
As You Like It.
Measure for Measure.
The Winter's Tale.
The Tempest.

(b) *Histories.*

Henry VIII.

(c) *Tragedies.*

Julius Cæsar.	Antony and Cleo-
Hamlet.	patra.
King Lear.	Troilus and Cressida.
Othello.	Macbeth.
Timon of Athens.	Cymbeline.
Pericles.	Coriolanus.

Shakespeare's career as a dramatist probably began with working over old plays.
Then he very likely turned his attention to
dramatizing popular novels and the stories of
the Chronicles. And it was only late in life
that he took the trouble to invent his own
plots. This may be accounted for by a number of reasons. Plays were demanded in
rapid succession. Older favorites were called
for, but with new embellishments. Freshness
of treatment rather than freshness of story
was expected. The popularity of the novels
translated from the Italian made their dramatization profitable.

Looking upon "Titus Andronicus" as an old
play simply retouched by Shakespeare, we
perceive that his first works were comedies
and histories, the sources of which were easily
obtainable from the Chronicles and Italian
novels, and the treatment of which by a

young poet of genius would naturally be happy. Previous to 1600 he composed but two tragedies proper, and only one of these, "Romeo and Juliet," has been accepted as entirely his own. This is the proper development. Comedy calls for less skill and experience in both matter and manner than tragedy, and serves to evolve the latent genius and strengthen the poet for the severer demands of the serious drama. It may be objected that "John" and "Richard III." are tragedies. But here much was supplied by history that could have been evolved otherwise only with long years of experience. And these tragic attempts of his early career, though wonderously rich in language and burning thoughts, show many faults of versification and construction not to be found in his later works. Rime, from which Shakespeare did not for a long time free himself, is particularly noticeable all through this first period, and while not inconsistent with the lighter work of comedy, is at variance with, and so, as a rule, offensive to, the spirit of tragedy. In Shakespeare's grandest tragedies, as "Macbeth" and "Antony and Cleopatra," there is almost a total absence of rime, being only used where it becomes at once an ornament and a necessity. All through this first period the freshness, boldness and light-heartedness of youth is constantly bubbling forth. There is a wild exuberance of fancy and imagination which nothing can restrain. Only age is able to check and hold this within its proper bounds.

Gradually the play-wright acquired a firm grasp on his subjects and a thorough mastery of his verse. Still he is loath to part with the loved excrescences of poetry, but they appear less frequently. What a wonderful advance in power and breadth of treatment from the " Comedy of Errors " and " Love's Labour's Lost " to the " Merchant of Venice " and " A Midsummer Night's Dream."

In the second period we are at once struck by the preponderance of tragedy. We have but one history, Henry VIII., and this by its treatment shows the poet to have grown rather weary of working over the English Chronicles. There is a decided tendency in it for the imagination to leave the region of the actual. And in the comedies likewise the sombre or the fantastical strive for place. "Twelfth Night " and " As You Like It," succeeding closely the " Midsummer Night's Dream," are permeated with the same idyllic character which was to reach its height in the "Tempest." In both is perceivable also the serious phase which becomes so comprehensive in " Measure for Measure " and " The Winter's Tale " as almost to remove them from the field of comedy. Shakespeare found now the proper scope for his developed powers to be afforded best by tragedy. Here he could depict heroic characters, gigantic sins and crimes and inmeasurable suffering. The legends and histories of the world were called upon to furnish him with themes upon which he should pour forth his majestic imagery and poetry. Roman history gave rise to what Ulrici has called the Roman cycle, viz.: "Coriolanus," "Julius Cæsar," "Antony and Cleopatra " and "Timon of Athens." "Pericles " and "Troilus and Cressida " came from the east. "Hamlet " and " Macbeth " from the north. "Othello " from the south. "Lear " and "Cymbeline " were indigenous. And of these nine are masterpieces of dramatic poetry.

In his comedies and tragedies Shakespeare's genius was ever on the ascending scale. The last were his greatest. In the historical plays, however, the height of this style is reached in Henry V. The remaining

plays are inferior to that in merit. And this
may be traced to a very apparent cause.
Ulrici has pointed out that each play was
given a central, life-bestowing idea ; that in
the working out of this there must be an increase in interest and in action, until the
climax, the catastrophe is reached, after
which there is necessarily a decrease of interest, and the chief object is to dispose of
affairs as rapidly and consistently as possible.
Now in the ten historical plays, while each is
complete in itself, yet they are all related to
one another, and go to make. up a grand
whole. That is, each has its own individual
permeating idea, but subservient to one
grand idea, which runs through them all,
connecting them as by a thread. Accepting
then the theory that these ten histories are
to be considered respectively as so many acts
of one great play, the central idea running
through them must ever increase in interest
and importance, until the climax is reached,
after which we hasten towards our conclusion.
This drama, whose central idea is the usurpa-
tion of the throne by the house of Lancaster,
has for its prologue " King John," and for its
epilogue " Henry VIII." The pinnacle of
fame for his house was reached in the glorious

reign of Henry V. From this all that followed was a rapid descent. A like effort has
been made to discover a connection between
the four tragedies, "Coriolanus," "Julius
Cæsar," "Antony and Cleopatra," and
"Timon of Athens," and a very ingenious
result has been obtained. Ulrici states
these plays to form a cycle, whose object is the representation of the rise and fall
of the Roman sovereignty. . "Coriolanus"
depicts the struggle between patricians and
plebeians. "Julius Cæsar," the destruction
of the republic. "Antony and Cleopatra,"
the victory of the empire. "Timon of
Athens," the corruption, which in its turn is
to destroy that empire.

Commentators on Shakespeare have so
diligently and perseveringly hunted out and
dug up every probable and possible bit of
material or matter which *might* have contributed to a portion of his works, or from
which he may have drawn an inspiration ;
they have pointed out so much in his plays
that he did *not* write that one is apt to pause
and wonder what he did write, and whether
this Shakespeare was the wonderful man we
have been taught to believe him, and wherein
lies the great service he has rendered English

literature, and why he should be considered the poet preëminent, if he is a vulgar plagiarist, who has given to the world nothing new, but has merely arranged his plays from matter that in one form or another was already in existence. Then must we, if possible, compare the sources with the plays themselves, and forgetting the critic and the commentator, try for ourselves to discover the essential difference. It will not be difficult. It lies in the difference between loose piles of brick and mortar and the palace, between the crude paints when in the pots and when on the canvas. The intellect of the architect, the hand of the artist. That is the difference. We are not indebted to Shakespeare for the brick and mortar, the paint and canvas he has used, but for the house he has built, the picture he has painted. He has breathed life into the otherwise well-nigh inanimate objects. When we begin to appreciate the spirit of his compositions, we understand wherein consists his greatness. True, a Juliet, a Rosalind, a Cleopatra existed in literature before Shakespeare wrote, but what lifeless creatures they are beside his immortal trio. A revengeful Jew, a melancholy Dane, a blindly fond father and king were to be found in literature, but no such Shylock, nor Hamlet, nor Lear. Holinshed, Stowe and Halle's Chronicles, Plutarch's Lives, Boccaccio's Decameron, Italian novels, English plays furnished Shakespeare only with skeletons which he did not hesitate to make use of, and clothe with flesh and blood.

In his comedies what infinite charm of poetry and poetic feeling! What delicate touches and what beautiful imagery! What sustained humor and exquisite lyrics! What sympathy with and understanding of character! And lastly what comprehensive treatment of the whole!

Ulrici makes two general groups of comedies under the heads of fancy and intrigue, according as the one or the other predominates. The comedies of fancy he places without the range of possibility although with its every seeming. And here he would range "Midsummer Night's Dream" with its fairies, "The Tempest" with its magic, "As You Like It," with its idyllic and impossible forest of Arden, "Twelfth Night," with its fantastic events. The second class, the comedy of intrigue, includes "Love's Labour's Lost" with its conflict of inclination and duties, "Comedy of Errors" with its bewildering

pairs of twins, " The Winter's Tale," " Measure for Measure " and " Merchant of Venice "
where life, honor and happiness are at stake.

In the comedies there is always depicted
the struggle of the real and the apparent,
with the final victory of the former.   In
" Love's Labour's Lost " it is the conflict between real and apparent inclinations, and it
is only when the king and his lords prove
false to their vows and true to their affections
that the play ends.   No close is possible to
the " Comedy of Errors " till the twins are
brought face to face and their actual identity
established.   Katherine and Petruchio, Beatrice and Benedict, Viola and Orsino, Hermione
and Perdita, Rosalind and Celia must dispense with their masks and become their
genuine selves ere the final curtain may drop.

Likewise Shakespeare is fond of contrasting characters.   Opposite the shrew he places
the master.   The faithful wife and the false
husband are confronted ; the virtuous maid
and the licentious suitor.   But the most beautiful contrast Ulrici has shown to be in " The
Merchant of Venice," which he says represents
human life as a great law-suit, with Shylock
impersonating revenge, and Portia mercy,
with the ultimate triumph of the latter.

> ". . . none of us
> Should see salvation ; we do pray for mercy.
> And that same prayer doth teach us all to render,
> The deeds of mercy—"

This contains the thought, the purpose of the whole play.

In this phase of the drama Shakespeare delights in making a woman the principal character, and what charming types does he present us ! The spoilt but magnificent Katherine ; the loving and devoted Helena ; the wise and womanly Portia ; the brilliant and sarcastic yet tender-hearted Beatrice ; the gentle but charming Viola ; that personification of caprice and mischief, Rosalind ; the faithful and suffering Hermione ; the noble and chaste Isabella. Nor are these women simply types of an age. They are types of womankind for all ages. Shakespeare perceived that woman with her natural tendency to intrigue, her capriciousness, rashness and inconsistency is especially suited to be the central figure about which a comedy may be composed.

It is worthy of note that the character of the clown, the court-fool, occurring so often in the comedies, is found in but one tragedy, King Lear, and here it is of great artistic value. This judicious use of a popular role is another proof of the master's skill and the fact that he worked by design and not, as some would have us believe by inspiration and chance.

In our admiration we must not be blind to defects, however. Even Shakespeare is not faultless, or rather the materials he used are not always perfect. We can not close our eyes to the disagreeable stories of " All's Well that Ends Well " and " Measure for Measure."

Nor can we feel satisfied with the termination of the latter piece. Poetical, if not . worldly, justice calls for a tragic end, or at least a severe punishment for Angelo. The separation of " The Winter's Tale " into two such distinct parts is undoubtedly a defect. So great a one in fact that in recent years but one great actress has deemed it suitable for the stage and successfully produced it. " The Merry Wives of Windsor " shows haste in construction and the treatment of Sir John Falstaff is widely at variance with the same character, as it occurs in Henry IV.

Of Shakespeare's maturest efforts, of his great tragedies, what can I say, what can any-one say, what is there left to be said ? Is it not enough to remark that since he dealt with the subjects, so enticing and full of interest to the dramatist, of the eleven tragedies of his second period but few have ever been handled by English play-wrights.

As women were the principal figures of his comedies, so are men of his tragedies. Their superior strength, greater opportunities, higher development, wider ambition, more brutal courage, made them naturally fitter objects for such a purpose. The deeply philosophical Hamlet, whose reason, not his irresolution, makes for him a hell of earth. Lear, the fond father, stubborn and blind he lives, blind and heart-broken he dies. Noble Othello, " whose hand, like the base Indian, threw a pearl away richer than all his tribe." Ambitious, bloody and conscience-stricken Macbeth, whose punishment while living leaves to that which may be hereafter but few horrors. Arrogant, haughty, heroic Coriolanus, that would not yield to the demands or prayers of a people, yet submitted to the voice of a woman. Antony, who sold the world for his mistress. Faithful Troilus, imperial Cæsar, subtle Cassius, noble Brutus. What a galaxy of giants! What a collection of heroes!

But though the interest is centered in man,

Shakespeare did not neglect the serious opportunities of woman, but has complemented his tragic picture of man with one of woman, which, if not equally great, fails, because of her nature, not because of the artist. Beside Hamlet we find the unfortunate Ophelia. By Lear is the beautiful Cordelia. Othello has his Desdemona, lovely in her innocence and sorrow. Cymbeline gives us Imogen. Coriolanus, Volumnia, the Roman matron. By Troilus is placed the false Cressida ; by Macbeth the majestic, star-aspiring, yet affectionate, Lady Macbeth. By Antony's side that most wonderful, most incomprehensible, most fascinating woman that ever existed in life or literature, Cleopatra. As she was, so Shakespeare paints her, or else she never was.

It has been objected to " Julius Cæsar " that the play falls with Cæsar's death into two parts, in the first of which we follow the fortunes of one hero, and in the latter of another. But this is, I think, quite erroneous. The hero of the play is not Cæsar, but Brutus, and it is his fortunes and his sufferings and his fall in which the interest is centered and upon which the drama is founded. Complaint has been made to Hamlet's so-called irresolution, but this is removed when we recognize the fact that it is not cowardly hesitancy, but philosophical weighing of right and wrong that restrains Hamlet from action, and it is only in momentary passion that he can possibly commit such a crime as murder. I have little liking for either " Timon of Athens," or " Pericles," and am quite willing to believe the critics, who state that Shakespeare's authorship is here doubtful, and is at best confined to certain passages.

In answer to the charge of immorality sometimes brought against our author, let us read what Coleridge says : " Shakespeare may sometimes be gross, but I boldly say that he is always moral and modest. Alas ! in our day decency of manners is preserved at the expense of morality of heart, and delicacies for vice allowed, while grossness against it is hypocritically, or at least morbidly, condemned." And this is the judgment of a man whose understanding of Shakespeare is unquestioned. Schlegel, the eminent German critic, says : " The objection that Shakespeare wounds our feelings by the open display of the most disgusting moral odiousness, unmercifully harrows up the mind, and tortures even our eyes by the exhibition of the most insupportable and hateful spectacles, is one of great and grave importance. He has, in fact, never varnished over wild and blood-thirsty passions with a pleasing exterior—never clothed crime and want of principle with a false show of greatness of soul ; and in that respect he is in every way deserving of praise. The reading, and still more the sight of some of his pieces, is not advisable to weak nerves any more than was the ' Eumenides,' of Aeschylus ; but is the poet who can only reach an important object by a bold and hazardous daring to be checked by consideration for such persons ? If effeminacy is to serve as a general standard of what tragical composition may properly exhibit to human nature, we shall be forced to set very narrow limits, indeed, to art, and the hope of anything like powerful effect must at once and forever be renounced." When we consider the plain speech customary in his age, and when we behold in the works of his contemporaries, predecessors and successors, a manner of language and thought unutterably vicious, we will no longer censure him on the moral score, but rather wonder at the purity and cleanness of such works as are beyond doubt his.

On the significance of the titles given his
plays much might be said. His histories
bear most properly the names of the different
reigns about which they treat. What images
are conjured up by the appellations Richard
II. and III., John, Henry IV. and VIII., and
how consistent are these images with the
plays for which the titles stand ! Notice the
brevity of the titles of the tragedies. Simply
a name or at most two. But by these names
are summoned up a whole world of thoughts
and feelings, deep, grand and terrible. Turn
to the comedies, and, on the contrary, what
long and fantastical headings?—" As You
Like It," " Twelfth Night, or What You ·
Will," " A Midsummer Night's Dream," " The
Tempest." Do not these names form indices
to all that follows ? Are we not sufficiently
prepared for intrigues, storms and mistakes
when we read the titles, " Merry Wives of
Windsor," " Taming of ·the Shrew," and
" Comedy of Errors ? " Even here as elsewhere nothing is left to chance, and all is
imbued with significance.

A list of the plays which have at one time
or another been ascribed to Shakespeare, but
all of which we can very safely refuse to
acknowledge as genuine, may be interesting :

"Thomas, Lord Cromwell," "Sir John Old-
castle," "The Yorkshire Tragedy," "Lo-
crine," "The London Prodigal," "The Puri-
tan," "The Two Noble Kinsmen," "The
Birth of Merlin," "The Merry Devil of
Edmonton," "Edward III.," "Mucedorus,"
"Arden of Feversham," "Alarum for Lon-
don," "Fair Em," "The Arraignment of
Paris," "The Double Falsehood," Dekker's
"Satiro-Mastix," "Wily Beguiled," "The
Tragical and Lamentable Murder of Master
George Saunders," Ford's "Lover's Melan-
choly," and Greene's "George-a-Greene,
Pinner of Wakefield."

During his life Shakespeare's plays were
remarkably popular, and enabled him to retire in comfort before old age overtook him.
Yet his great genius was really recognized
by only a few patrons and some of his literary
contemporaries, chiefly dramatists. Of his
thirty-seven plays only eighteen were published before his death, the first collection
seven years afterwards in 1623.

With the growth of Puritanism Shakespeare's fame waned, and with the Revolution
all representations ceased. However, Shakespeare was not forgotten, as he still continued
to reign in the hearts of the people supreme.

The Restoration revivified the well-nigh lifeless drama, and the stage again became an important factor in the life of the people. The strong characters in Shakespeare's plays made them attractive to ambitious actors, and once more they were performed.

But unfortunately, the false taste acquired from the French, caused them to be looked upon as remarkable, but exceedingly faulty, productions, and managers, actors and authors did not hesitate to adapt, re-arrange, *improve* and generally mutilate them. Dryden, D'Avenant, Granville, D'Urfey, Lacy, etc., were foremost in this ghoulish work. We find even the titles changed. "Cymbeline" becomes "The Injured Princess, or The Fatal Wager"; "Antony and Cleopatra," "All for Love"; "The Merry Wives of Windsor," "The Comical Gallant, or The Amours of Sir John Falstaff." But the most remarkable transformation was when John Lacy dubbed "Taming of the Shrew," "Sauny the Scot," and changed *Grumio* into a Scotchman, and the verse of the play into prose.

Sometimes changes were made more intelligently, and with more show of reason, as when Colley Cibben altered "Richard III." to suit the requirements of the remodeled stage. Gen-

erally only the most effective passages were
left untouched, but the editors did not hesitate to expunge what they deemed Shakespeare's harshnesses and excrescences. Powerful scenes were toned down and diluted. Tenderness was intensified and additional grossness bestowed upon the comic characters.

After the Stuarts were expelled, the king and
people withdrew their favor from the exces-
sively licentious drama, and foreign plays
and models came into vogue. The Italian
Opera was introduced. Corneille, Racine
and Molière were translated and imitated.
Addison's " Cato " appeared.

But in all merely imitative literary periods
attention and study is directed to former
achievements, and that is what occurred in
William's reign. Nicholas Rowe, and then
Pope, edited Shakespeare's plays, and a fresh
impetus was given to his popularity. Gradually actors, managers and learned men, came
to understand the greatness and worth of our
dramatist. Editions rapidly followed one
another. The attention of other nations was
attracted to the works of a man whom they
deemed a kind of savage genius.

But the greatest impulse to an appreciation of Shakespeare was given by an actor,

David Garrick. During his management of Drury Lane (1747–1776) he produced in the original texts twenty-four of Shakespeare's works, and appeared himself in seventeen different Shakespearean characters. Although he is not free from the charge of mutilating the plays in some degree, yet Garrick performed an invaluable benefit to the drama and to literature in reviving the original works, and in spreading broadcast a profound admiration and respect for our greatest dramatist and poet.

However, it was not until the early part of this century that Shakespeare came to be regarded in his true light, from a literary point of view. Before Coleridge English writers generally had criticized unmercifully the construction, the non-observance of unities, the moral tone, the verbiage and the grossness to be found in Shakespeare's works.

But Coleridge in England, Hugo in France, Lessing, Schlegel, Tieck and Ulrici in Germany, soon proved that Shakespeare had been entirely misunderstood and that he is guilty of few, if any, of the sins accounted to him. Since then all study of our author has been accompanied by veneration, and instead of willfully mutilating and mercilessly criticizing, editors now labor to restore and elucidate his texts.

His works in part or in whole have been translated into Italian, Portugese, Danish, Swedish, Dutch, Frisian, Bohemian, Hungarian, Wallachian, "Moslem Greek," Polish, Russian and Bengalee. Truly, Shakespeare is not the mouth-piece of simply one people, but of the whole civilized world.

IV.

JONSON AND HIS CONTEMPORARIES.

THE Elizabethan drama is the phenomenon of English and the marvel of every other literature. It is seldom in the history of literary activity that so much finds expression in so short a time. The half century which the years 1590 and 1640 includes, is the period which embraces the greatest names and marks the greatest epoch of the English drama. It is the period which produced more than forty poets, ten of whom are of superior rank and one the most admirable, possibly, that the world has ever known. It was a time when men felt deeply, believed blindly, loved passionately and expressed themselves boldly. Nothing was too sacred or profane, too delicate or too coarse, too tender or too brutal for these Titans of the theatre to depict. Man they dissected and mercilessly revealed his passions, emotions, sentiments, actions as they found them, good or bad ; oftener good and bad, for they did not hesitate to represent the real man, that mixture of nobility and baseness, strength and weakness. Of their works it has been said that, " The plays of the least known writers of that time are more remarkable than the most celebrated of all the succeeding times." And while this is an extreme view, and one that I do not think we should wholly concur in, it is to a certain extent true. The Elizabethan poets produced hundreds of pieces, fifty at least of which we may rank as masterpieces. There was no province of history or imagination that their genius did not compass and, freed from restraint, there was little that they did not attempt. Tragedy, comedy, romantic and domestic drama, chronicle histories, all filled with truthful and living portraits and details, reflecting the mind and manners of their age and nation. In this literature we find much that is gross and repulsive, much that to us seems shockingly immoral, much that indicates the decline of the drama. But the whole period is marked by vigor, genius and a genuine moral purpose. Wrong is invariably punished. If vice is depicted, it is to disgust, not to inflame. The fundamental idea is unobjectionable, however worthy of condemnation we may find the execution.

Of the master poet, Shakespeare, we have already spoken. We have now to deal with his contemporaries and immediate successors. Many of these whose names and works are obscured by the greater lights of their time we will barely mention. Our space is too limited to do otherwise. The more important writers, embracing some dozen names, we must more closely observe. One man, by his talents, industry and the judgment of posterity, has been placed above the rest.

BENJAMIN, or, as he preferred to be called, BEN JONSON, was born in 1573, a month after his father's decease. His mother subsequently re-married. Her second husband was a bricklayer, and, despite tradition, there is no reason to believe was otherwise than kind to Jonson. The family was poor, and lived in London, near Charing Cross. Jonson attended in his childhood a private school in the neighborhood. Afterwards he was sent to Westminster school, a friend, the famous antiquary Camden, sustaining the expense. For this Camden was repaid by Jonson's life-long gratitude. From Westminster it is said that our poet went to St. John's College, Cambridge, but there is no authority which substantiates the statement. Later in life both universities conferred upon him the degree of Master of Arts, which he modestly says was done "by their favor, not my studies." This, however, is not the case, for although his studies may not have been conducted at or under the guidance of the universities, still the unusual amount and quality of learning he acquired fully entitled him to the honors given. His natural taste for study, fortified by Camden's good schooling, enabled him to accomplish a vast amount of literary research and labor.

When Jonson returned from school to London, he was for a short time employed in his stepfather's trade of bricklaying. This being distasteful to him, he entered the army, and served in a campaign in the Low Countries. He seems to have remained abroad only a short time. Soon after his return he married, and began to write for the stage. His wife, he told Drummond, was "a shrew, but honest." For five years they lived apart. They had several children, the eldest of whom died in 1603, in his eighth year.

Like most of the great dramatists of his time, much that we have concerning Jonson's life is untrustworthy, particularly that which refers to the period before 1597. In that year he is recorded as being a member of Henslowe's company. Acting and play-writing appears to have been uphill work for him at first. In 1598, if not before, " Every Man in His Humour," perhaps Jonson's best comedy, was produced, and his success assured. His unfortunate duel with Gabriel Spenser, in 1598, in which he killed Spenser, interrupted for a time his brilliant career. Jonson was thrown into prison, and while there became a Roman Catholic, which he remained for twelve years. At the expiration of this time he underwent a second conversion.

No charges of insincerity or weakness should be brought against Jonson in consequences of his changes of faith, for they were undoubtedly the result of conviction. Rather by his courage to follow his belief does he deserve our admiration, and the right to the title he was so proud of—an honest man.

From his imprisonment in consequence of the duel with Spenser, he was released in a few months. Afterward he must have experienced sore poverty, as but little money, less than £200 in all, was brought him by his plays. But with the advent of the Stuarts, Jonson's fortunes were bettered. " The Masque," a species of literature in which he

has been surpassed by but one author, gave a
new direction to his talents. They introduced him to royal favor and crowned him
with success. His collaborator in this domain was the celebrated Inigo Jones, a man
with whom he afterwards quarreled.

In 1616 a pension of one hundred marks was
conferred upon him, which Charles I. later
made as many pounds. Every first day of
the new year the Earl of Pembroke, a famous
patron of letters, sent Jonson £20 with which
to buy books. With another patron, Esmé
Stuart, Lord d'Aubigny, he dwelt five years.
In 1613 he went to France as governor of one
of the sons of Sir Walter Raleigh, then a state-
prisoner in the Tower. During his sojourn
in Paris he made the acquaintance of Cardinal de Perron and took occasion in his usual
frank manner to inform the Cardinal concerning that gentleman's translation of Virgil,
that " they were naught." In 1618–19 he made
a journey to Scotland and spent some time
with the poet Drummond, who has left some
very interesting " Conversations " with Jonson.

Our poet was fond of wine, tobacco
and good company. His nature was com-
bative. This finally got him into trouble

with Dekker and Marston, both of whom had
been his collaborators at an earlier date.
They believed Jonson to have satirized them
and they assailed him. He hotly responded.
"The Poetaster" from Jonson, the "Satiromastix" of Dekker, are the chief monu-
ments of this dispute. Reaching a climax in
the "Satiromastix," it ceased for some years.

In 1625 Jonson again began to write for the
stage, but with only mediocre success. His
imprudent life brought in time debt and dis-
ease to trouble him. His later plays, several
of which were written on a sick bed, show
plainly his waning powers as a dramatist.
An unfinished pastoral drama, "The Sad
Shepherd," proves, however, that his poetic
faculty was unimpaired to the last. He died
August 6th, 1635.

The greater part of Jonson's life was spent
in poverty, and like many other great men
when wealth came, he knew not how to preserve it. His jovial life at the Mermaid Inn,
and later at the Devil Tavern, is well known.
His chief characteristics were combativeness,
frankness and self-consciousness. He was
entirely aware of his own worth. Though he
wrote for, he despised the stage. It is to be
feared, however, that his scorn was born of

his failures to please. He was never a great favorite as a dramatist, though some of his plays met with considerable success. He presumed too much in his faith in his own intelligence, and the public's depraved taste and ignorance. Nevertheless, he was a poet of great moral courage and intellectual power. He cared little for the approbation of the general public, but was most anxious for that of the judicious. He had warm friends and bitter enemies. His quarrels with his literary associates were manifold. In his old age he was regarded justly as the chief of the literary world, and his death was sincerely lamented by his friends. Jonson was possessed of a great memory and remarkable learning. His works are easily classified as tragedies, comedies and masques; all of which show laborious and conscientious research, great vigor, wonderful skill in construction and characterization, but are deficient in soul—that attractive but indefinable something we most long for in poetry. It is said that Jonson wrote all his verses first in prose.

Neither of his historical tragedies, "Sejanus" and "Catiline," achieved great success. They are too ponderous, too much taken up with accuracy of det ils and too little given to spontaneity. We find an abundance of classical knowledge, but not that delicate perception of character of which Shakespeare was the master. Jonson either under or overdraws his portraits. He has left but two tragedies, though a third, "The Fall of Mortimer," was sketched.

From the long list of Jonson's comedies we will select his most characteristic and celebrated ones : " Every Man in His Humour," " The Poetaster," " Epicoene," " Volpone, the Fox." The first named made his reputation as a dramatist. The two last firmly maintained it. The second is his famous satirical contribution to his dispute with Marston and Dekker.

" Every Man in His Humour " is a play in Jonson's happiest vein, with a slight plot, characters marked and real, the central idea of which is that every human fault is curable by excess. It is a comedy of character, and much superior, though not so elaborate as its companion piece, "Every Man Out of His Humour." It was produced at least by 1598.

" Volpone, the Fox," printed in 1607, is a moral satire. It is one of Jonson's most powerful and successful efforts. The picture

of the depravity of his age is no doubt a faithful, though revolting one, and while one perceives the bitter attack made by the dramatist
upon immorality and the commendable purpose that inspired the composition, yet, he
can not look with pleasure upon its scenes.
Nevertheless, it is an admirable achievement.

"Epicoene, or The Silent Woman," has
been called Jonson's most entertaining
comedy. One might not improperly speak
of it as a farce. An old misanthrope, who
hates noise, marries what he believes to be a
silent woman, but who, immediately after
the ceremony, proves to be a talkative crea-
ture, ultimately turning out to be a boy. The
fun is brisk, situations effective, and the
interest grows with each succeeding act, the
climax being reached towards the close of
the last. Jonson was not less scrupulous in
his observance of the unities of time and
action here than elsewhere.

Jonson's comedies were imitative of the
Latin models, "Terence" and "Plautus;"
satirical in tone, and written for the purpose
of representing and correcting follies and
vices. In the "Alchemist" he attacks a
whilom pest of society, and did no little good

towards ridding the world of it. " Bartholo-
mew Fair" assails the Puritans, and is a
perfect dictionary of slang. " Volpone"
belabors contemporary vice. And so on.
Unfortunately Jonson's characters are at
times too grotesque, and too laboriously
constructed. The author burdens himself
with science and theories, and allows his
critical sense to mar his artistic feeling. His
later works, "The New Inn" (1629) and
"The Magnetic Lady" (1632), show the
decadence of his powers, and were not
successful. "The Tale of a Tub" (1633) met
with a somewhat better fate.

As a writer of masques no one has been so
successful or so prolific as Ben Jonson.
Accurate learning, great inventive power,
and considerable originality are the requisites
for an author of masques. All of these
qualities Jonson possessed in a large degree.
As regards acquired powers, scholarship,
he was infinitely better equipped than any
other Elizabethan writer. His experience and
knowledge of man and life was wide and
varied. His idea of his task was noble. His
chief merit, conception and reproduction of
character. Add to this the fact that character,
not action, is the essential thing in a masque,

and we understand why Jonson excells in this particular field. The masques of " Blackness," " The Satyr " and " The Penates " are three of great beauty, chosen at random where all are excellent. The first-named had the honor of being impersonated by the Queen and her ladies at Whitehall, on Twelfth Night, 1605.

The Pastoral Play, of which dramatic species Jonson has left us one exquisite, though unfinished example, " The Sad Shepherd," is the bucolic idyl in a dramatic form. This admits of the introduction of both mythological and allegorical elements. It flourished in Italy towards the close of the fifteenth century, when Poliziano's " Orfeo " appeared. The artificial character of the Pastoral, permitting the display of classical learning and scope for the imagination and compliment, thinly veiled by allegory, commended it for imitation to our Elizabethan poets, and its influence is perceptible throughout the drama, particularly in comedy. The chief objection to the Pastoral Play is its hovering between artificiality and burlesque. The entire conception of such a combination of rustic simplicity and poetical manners is foreign to the modern mind. Of the Elizabethan productions in this domain Fletcher's "Faithful Shepherdess" is the most noteworthy.

GEORGE CHAPMAN (1557 or 9–1634) is a worthy representative of a certain class of writers whose inventive powers are good, but who are too much given to narration, to rhetoric and to verbiage. The greatest strength of this class of writers consists in individual passages which are often of great beauty. Chapman's best works are those written in conjunction with other authors, as was then the custom. He did not produce a single striking female character. Like Jonson, his learning is constantly appearing. "The Blind Beggar of Alexandria," "Cæsar and Pompey," "Byron's Conspiracy," "Bussy D'Ambois," and "The Revenge of Bussy D'Ambois," are some of his works. Marston and Jonson assisted him in the composition of "Eastward Ho," that endeavor which imprisoned its authors and for a time threatened their destruction ; and Shirley was a collaborator in the production of "Chabot, Admiral of France." Chapman was a learned and traveled gentleman, of excellent character, and enjoyed the friendship of all his contemporaries. He held a high position as a dramatist and writer of

masques, but is even better known as a trans-
lator of Homer.   He died when nearly
eighty years old.

THOMAS DEKKER is probably more famous
as the man who led the attack against Jonson,
in that celebrated quarrel which produced
" The Poetaster," and " The Satiromastix,"
than as an author of special merit.   Yet he
occupies a conspicuous place as a comic
dramatist.   Possessed of humor, pathos,
poetical ability, yet lacking in that vigorous
imagination, progressive spirit and high
moral sense which enable a writer to influence his age.   He collaborated so much
that his own work is with difficulty recognized.   Middleton, Chettle, Haughton, Webster, Massinger, Ford, Day, etc., are writers
who assisted in his compositions.   Dekker
was born in London, and there he lived,
worked and died.   He was a prolific and
hasty writer, often gross.   None of his plays
are of a high order, nor have any claim to
great artistic excellence.   A list of the plays
in which he was concerned would include
" The Shoemaker's Holiday," " Old Fortu-
natus," " Satiromastix," " Patient Grissil,"
" The Roaring Girl," " The Witch of Edmonton," etc.

Of JOHN MARSTON'S, personal life little is known. It was his play " Antonio and Mellida " which Jonson ridiculed in " The Poetaster." Marston achieved only partial success in his more ambitious works, as his tragedies. In a less pretentious vein as in " Eastward Ho " he is more fortunate. He was talented, possessed some humor, pathos and poetic ability, but his individual works often betray a false tone.

THOMAS MIDDLETON (1570–1627), like Dekker, had no hesitancy in collaborating with his fellow dramatists. He produced works in conjunction with Rowley, Henslowe, Dekker, etc. He was a university man. As an author he was easy, fluent, free from bombast, prolific, a faithful reflector of the common, never the exceptional, traits of the people of his time. Of these, and for these, he wrote, his plays being singularly uninteresting to a modern reader. He is inferior in brilliancy and depth of feeling to his contemporaries, but free from the exaggeration to which many of them are so prone. There is a pleasing rapidity of action in his plays, which usually contain two plots drawn in the customary indelicate manner. In 1624 his best known work, a comedy, " The Game of Chess," was produced, and after a successful run of nine days was prohibited by command of the King. The Spanish Ambassador was offended at the representation of his sovereign on the stage, particularly the manner of representation, for the English people were not at this time friendly to Spain, and the English dramatist had not been uninfluenced in his play by this fact. There was a law by which the representing of a modern Christian king on the stage was forbidden, so the obnoxious play was prohibited. Middleton and the players escaped punishment, however, owing to the public sentiment being so much in concurrence with that of his play.

THOMAS HEYWOOD (1570 circ.–1650) is the typical play-wright, but not a great poet. His plays were written to be acted, rather than read, and embrace every species. Tieck styles him "the model of a light and rapid talent." He is said to have been the author of or collaborator in over two hundred plays, besides many other works, as romances, pageants, and translations. He is not a writer of the first rank, despite his astonishing productivity. He shows considerable pathos, some humor, and great skill in constructing situations and startling climaxes. It was this last quality that made his plays successful. His best plays are " A Woman Killed with Kindness " and "The Fair Maid of the West."

Amongst thirty authors noted by Henslowe as receiving pay for plays between the years 1598–1601, we notice the names of SAMUEL ROWLEY and WILLIAM ROWLEY, who were collaborators with many prominent Elizabethan dramatists. Also WENTWORTH SMITH, " A man fortunate in his initials "; GEORGE WILKINS, RICHARD HATHAWAY, and other lesser lights.

A number of anonymous plays belonging to this period must not escape mention. Their merit, however, is not great. " The Life and Death of Jack Straw," " A Knave to Knowe a Knave," and " Looke About You," are three worthiest of notice.

Despite the popularity and greatness of the drama of the Elizabethan Theatre, there still existed a set of writers hostile to the English dramatic development, and who opposed it, in a feeble manner, by plays written with a totally different purpose. SAMUEL DANIEL and WILLIAM ALEXANDER, EARL OF STERLING, were chief amongst these. Daniel, by his prose and sonnets, shows himself to have been a writer of merit, but he was a pseudo·

classicist, and did not possess much dramatic
power. "Philotas," "Cleopatra" and "The
Queen's Arcadia," are some of Daniel's plays.
Sterling was inferior to and even more
foreign than Daniel in his compositions.

Also many plays continued for some time
to be written for the Court, houses of nobility
and the Universities. But these finally disappeared before the steady growth of the
popular theatre.

Among Shakespeare's contemporaries there
are but three whose popularity rivaled his in
his own time, or to whom fame has assigned
places near him in later days : Jonson, Beaumont and Fletcher. It is even probable that
the last-named authors were more admired in
the Elizabethan, and undoubtedly they were
in the Restoration period, than the master
poet. During the commonwealth it was their
plays, or scenes from their plays that were
given at fairs, in halls, taverns and on mounte-
bank's stages. Some players were giving sur-
reptitiously a tragedy of Fletcher's at the
Cock-pit shortly before the execution of
Charles I., when the performance was interrupted and the players arrested for breach of
the peace. But with the progress of thought
and culture, Beaumont and Fletcher's fame

declined. Gradually they came to be classed
as inferior to Shakespeare, and before the
eighteenth century had closed they were
being laid aside because of the impurity and
grossness of which in their own time they had
deemed themselves the reformers. As criticism became broader and higher, their plays
were found lacking in what Schlegel calls
" high seriousness," and we would denomi-
nate as true artistic feeling. To-day there is
not a single work of these famous authors on
the boards. Indeed, despite the fact of their
past glory and their unquestioned merit, a
revival of their fame has been long delayed
and scarcely in keeping with their deserts.

Although the collaboration of dramatists is
one of the most ordinary phenomena, especially of the Elizabethan period, there is no
instance so famous in the history of literature
as that of Beaumont and Fletcher. As a rule,
where two or more authors are concerned in
the production of the same work, there is a
consciousness, often manifest evidence of
piece-meal efforts. This is remarkable by its
absence in the plays of our twin poets. So
much so that it is with extreme difficulty that
scholars have attempted to separate their
work, and often the task has been given up as

hopeless. The two men were joined by many circumstances ; gentle birth, university education, nearness of age, similarity of thought and taste, affected by the same literary influences, the originality of neither so great as to brook no interference. The chief differences were merely external ones. Fletcher being urged ever to greater activity by his poverty, Beaumont never experiencing that unpleasant stimulus. So that while choice was for Beaumont the only incentive to write, Fletcher was urged, no doubt, as strenuously by necessity. Yet, there was never a greater harmony of thought between two men. In the selection and treatment of a subject there does not seem to have been a difference, and it is not strange, therefore, that they should come to be regarded as *one author.* It is remarkable that when working alone Fletcher shows no peculiarities not to be found in his joint compositions. He seems neither to have been impeded nor assisted, as regards meritorious work, by the collaboration of Beaumont.

JOHN FLETCHER was several years older than his co-laborer. He was the younger son of a large family. His father had held successively the positions of President of Bene't

(now Corpus Christi) College, Cambridge ;
minister of Rye, in Sussex, where John was
born, December, 1579 ; Dean of Peterborough,
in which capacity he attended Mary, Queen
of Scots, in Fotheringay Castle, and endeavored to persuade her to recant the
Catholic faith ; Bishop of Bristol and Bishop
of London. While holding the last-named
position he died, leaving a large family and a
heavy debt.

Of John Fletcher's early life little has been
ascertained. Being a younger son his pros-
pects could not have been bright, and at his
father's death his inheritance was probably
confined to an equal half of the Bishop's
library. This was an undoubted recognition
of the literary tastes Fletcher had early displayed, and which he inherited, as his father,
uncle and cousins, Phineas and Giles, were all
men of letters. The two last particularly
having won honorable places for themselves
in English literature. In 1591, and again in
1593, we have evidence showing him to have
been at Bene't College, Cambridge. From
that time, until we find him connected with
the London stage, nothing is known of his
proceedings. His first plays, written in conjunction with Beaumont, were not successful.

"Philaster," produced in 1608–9, was, however, and from that time neither Beaumont
nor Fletcher had just cause to complain of
the lack of popular approval. After Beaumont's death, in 1616, Fletcher continued to
write for the stage, often associating himself
with other dramatists, as Massinger, William
Rowley and others. He was admired and
beloved by his fellows, and is said to have
ended his days without an enemy. He was
witty, modest, disliked flattery, but honestly
loved well-earned applause. He was a gentleman by birth, breeding and conduct. He
died August, 1625, a victim of the plague,
and was buried at St. Saviours, Southwark,
where, unfortunately, no trace has been left
of his grave.

FRANCIS BEAUMONT was born at Grace-
Dieu, in Leicestershire, the home of his ancestors. His family was ancient and his father
was a Justice of the Common Pleas. His
elder brother, John, also won some reputation
as a poet. Francis, after a short residence at
Broadgates Hall, Oxford, entered the Inner
Temple in 1600, with which society he preserved his connections, though he soon turned
his attentions from law to literature. He became acquainted with Ben Jonson, and their

friendship was life-long. A stronger intimacy was presently formed, however, with John Fletcher, with whom his name will be forever linked. Beaumont does not seem to have written anything alone, save a few poems, which are not remarkable, except as proofs of his having continued a member of the society into which he was born. Brought into contact with the stage by Jonson and Fletcher, he must have imbibed a warm love for it, as there can be no other reason for the habits of life ascribed by tradition to Beaumont and Fletcher, as the former inherited a part of his elder brother's property in 1606, and was never in want. In 1613 he married a lady of birth and fortune, Ursula Isley, which event must have changed his mode of life, and interfered somewhat with his relations to Fletcher. Nevertheless they continued to collaborate until Beaumont's death in 1616, which event was sincerely mourned by many contemporaries. As an author Beaumont is rated as inferior to Fletcher in genius, as he certainly was in productivity. For a long time the two men when at work on a play, are said to have been associated in the most intimate personal intercourse. They lived together not far from the play-house, and had everything in common, "even the same clothes and cloakes."

Fletcher's plays fall naturally into three classes, (1) those written in conjunction with Beaumont ; (2) those written alone ; (3) those written with the assistance of other dramatists.

The first joint works of Beaumont and Fletcher, " The Woman Hater " and " Thierry and Theodoret," were failures, as we have before remarked. In 1608, however, " Philaster " was produced, which was exceedingly popular. This play may be taken as representative of the colabor of our two poets. " Philaster " contains much pathos and beauty of language, characters and situations. There is a suggestion of " Hamlet " in the hero at first, and a striking resemblance to Shakespeare's Viola in " Euphrasia-Bellario," though the latter is not so happy in her ultimate fate as the heroine of " Twelfth Night." There is some exquisite poetry in this piece, which might be called a tragicomedy. Among other successful efforts may be named the mock-heroic drama, ":The Knight of the Burning Pestle " ; the vigorous and interesting " Knight of Malta," and that source of much dispute as to merit, " The

Maid's Tragedy." The last-named was
prohibited under Charles II., but re-written
by Sheridan Knowles, was acted, as late as
1837, by the tragedian Macready. It contains
two central figures, Evadne, a terrible character, and Melanthius, a noble one. Nevertheless, the play is loathsome to modern
tastes.

Of the plays assigned to Fletcher alone,
his pastoral drama, "The Faithful Shepherdess" (1610), and the comedy "The
Woman's Prize, or The Tamer Tamed"
(1625), deserve special mention. The former
on account of its being the highest achievement in the pastoral drama in our literature.
Notwithstanding the high estimation in which
it is held, criticism does not deem it to have
escaped the usual dangers attendant on this
species, sameness and artificiality. The
beauties are those of detail and diction.
"The Woman's Prize, or The Tamer Tamed,"
is to be remarked as an attempt in a direction
seldom ventured by a play-wright. Fletcher's
object was to use, and, if possible, surpass
the success of Shakespeare's "Taming of the
Shrew," by writing a companion piece, or
epilogue, to that famous comedy. His effort
was, for the time being, successful. Indeed,

it is reported that Shakespeare's play on being given at Court was "likt," but Fletcher's, given five days afterwards, was "very well likt." Undoubtedly it is a clever comedy, though far inferior to its predecessor.

Amongst the group of plays, assigned as the result of the co-labor of Fletcher and contemporaries other than Beaumont, are "The Two Noble Kinsmen," a portion of which has been attributed by some critics to Shakespeare ; "Love's Pilgrimage," a joint work with Shirley ; "The Queen of Corinth," in which Massinger's hand is traced, and "The Bloody Brother," the joint author of which is unknown. In this last-named play there are passages and whole scenes of a most beautiful and highly developed style, but, unfortunately, a large part is inartistic, and the working out of the plot unsatisfactory. There is a noticeable and lamentable . unevenness in this tragedy, whose opening is so promising and the close of which is so disappointing. The character of the mother, from the commanding position she at first assumes, sinks into insignificance as the play progresses.

The chief facts to be noted in a study of Beaumont and Fletcher, some of which they have in common with other Elizabethan dramatists, are :

(1) Their remarkable productivity. Their works comprise fifty-two plays.

(2) The advantages they derived from their birth, breeding, education, friends, and the time at which they lived.

(3) The unusually wide range of subjects handled, which undoubtedly was the result of their education that had familiarized them with history, philosophy, classic and modern literature.

(4) Their exceeding popularity, which was in part due to intrinsic merit, in part to the fact that they adapted themselves to the tastes and tendencies of their age, unfortunately not a great one. James I. did not inspire the chivalric loyalty and noble sentiments which Elizabeth had done. What was impulsively consecrated to her was granted indifferently, and as a matter of course, to him. The poets, particularly Beaumont and Fletcher, everywhere express an unshaken faith in "the divine right of kings."

(5) Great moral defects and grossness, a most lamentable stain on their poetic renown, are visible in nearly all, if not all, their works. They seem to have no conception of feminine

purity. This immorality is the more griev-
ous, since Beaumont and Fletcher were un-
conscious of it and believed themselves to be
reformers. It is a manifest sign of the
depravity of the times.

(6) As regards their literary qualities we
find their construction to be light, at times
skillful ; clever in adapting ; happy in their
characterization within certain limits ; excelling in the brilliancy and fluency of their
poetry and in their pathos ; as a rule free
from bombast ; lacking in tragic and moral
elevation ; sometimes extravagant in their
conceptions. Fletcher was the superior artist
in versification, his peculiarity being sweetness rather than firmness.

(7) That their plays are wonderfully brilliant and theatrical, but superficial, unnatural, corrupt and unsatisfactory.

We have now to speak of a genius of surpassing and original, though not versatile
powers, JOHN WEBSTER. Little has been ascertained of his life, nor is it known when he
died. He began his career as a dramatist in
1601, when Henslowe mentions a play by
Webster, entitled " The Gwisse." He seems
to have co-operated with Dekker, Marston,
Ford, Rowley, etc., with all of whom he

appears to have been on the best of terms. It is to be regretted that so few of the plays of which he was the sole author have been preserved. " The Duchess of Malfi," a superb, though terrible tragedy, is generally conceded to be his masterpiece. Other notable plays in which . Webster was concerned are " Vittoria Corombona, or, The White Devil," and " Appius and Virginia."

The characteristics of this remarkable genius are :

(1) His apparent disposition and extraordinary ability to accumulate murders, suicides and executions, thus showing a love for the horrible.

(2) His elaborate investigation of the terrible side of human nature, and of bloody deeds.

(3) Possessed of fine poetic feeling, and capable of forming strong situations, but lacking a high moral purpose and ability to construct.

(4) His characters are possible, but abnormal.

Taine says, " Webster is a sombre man whose thoughts seem incessantly to be haunting tombs and charnel houses. . . No one has equaled him in creating desperate characters,

utter wretches, bitter misanthropes, in black-
ening and blaspheming human life, in depicting the shameless depravity and refined fero-
city of Italian manners."

There are few names in our dramatic literature that are entitled to, or that receive more
respect, than that of PHILIP MASSINGER, one of
the secondary stars of the later Elizabethan
drama.   He was born at Salisbury in 1584,
and was the son of a gentleman attached to
the service of the Earl of Pembroke, for
whose family he ever entertained the warmest gratitude. He was university bred, a
Roman Catholic of unusual religious piety,
moderate and, liberal in political views and a
man of considerable reading.   He was often
in the extremest poverty during his London
career, and was twice obliged to appeal for
monetary aid. A number of Massinger's
plays fell victim to "Warburton's Cook,"
that is, Somerest Herald's cook, who used his
collection of MSS. as coverings for her pastry.
Still a considerable portion of Massinger's
works have been saved, carefully edited, and
exhaustively criticised. "The Virgin Martyr"
(a joint work), "The Duke of Milan," "The
Picture," "The City Madam," "The Bond-
man" (one of Massinger's best and most pop-

ular efforts), "The Roman Actor" (a meritorious drama and its author's favorite), and
"The New Way to Pay Old Debts," are his
most celebrated plays. The last-named is
acknowledged, I believe, by all critics to be
his master-piece ; certainly it has been the
most popular and enduring.

This unvarying success has been attributed,
doubtless with considerable truth, to the
remarkable central character, Sir Giles Overreach, and the strong didactic element
clothed in striking rhetoric. Yet, despite this
effective combination of attractive theatrical
elements, the moral tone and noble purpose
of the play should have given it success, and
certainly do give it a high place in the dramatic literature of the day. The play is
original in construction, and in the central
figure, while the others are of sufficient dignity and individuality to deserve praise. Sir
Giles Overreach is a picture of incarnate
evil. His nature is revealed by effective and
contrasting situations. He is depicted with
unusual dramatic force, and his punishment
is commensurate with his guilt. It is the
portrait of a grasping, grinding, ambitious,
moneyed man of the world. Massinger
delights in depicting the conflict between

right and wrong, lust and chastity ; the forti-
tude bestowed by conviction and conscience ;
the self-punishment of crime ; woman's pure
self-sacrifice ; the nobility of self-control.
Yet, notwithstanding his eloquent and pleasing verse, his skill in the choice and execution
of his work, he has many faults.   Ward says,
his characters seem labeled, and there is no
mistaking them as *dramatis personæ*, though
we have some difficulty in understanding
them as human beings.   Nevertheless, Massinger's plays form an honorable monument
to an honorable dramatist.

NATHANIEL FIELD (1590–1640) was a companion of Massinger's in his poverty.   He
was a good actor, and as a dramatist shows a
curious combination of skill and recklessness,
which fact his checquered career may explain.
" A Woman is a Weather-cock," and "Amends
for Ladies," are his two extant plays.

JOHN FORD (1586–1640 circ.) was the second
son of a Devonshire gentleman of position.
Ford's first appearance as an author was made
in 1616 with the elegiac poem, " Fame's Memo-
rial."   Shortly afterwards he commenced his
career as a dramatist, and during it enjoyed
the patronage of several men of rank and
wealth.   The earliest of his published plays

was "The Lover's Melancholy" (1629). Of
his other works, "The Witch of Edmonton,"
in which Dekker and William Rowley were
also concerned, we have before mentioned;
"The Broken Heart" and "Perkin Warbeck" deserve notice. The last-named is a
chronicle history of great merit, and is one of
the few that bear comparison with the Shakespeare series. Ford occupies an entirely distinct place amongst our dramatists. He is
strangely devoid of humor. Gifford speaks
of his comedians in one play as a "despic-
able set of buffoons." They are invariably
gross, brutal and contemptible. An exception should be made for the single character
of John-a-Water, the truism-loving Mayor
of Cork, in "Perkin Warbeck." Ford's re-
deeming qualities are his admirable verse,
sweet, fluent and strong; his lyrical gifts; his
unsurpassed tenderness; his magical changes
from raging passion to delicate touches of
thrilling sweetness; his ability to portray the
depths of passion, sorrow and despair. But
once again we are called upon to regret that
such admirable powers should have been
expended upon such disgusting materials.
His plots and characters are revolting. It
was such writers as Ford that by their

very genius hastened the decay of the drama.

JAMES SHIRLEY (1596–1666) was a Londoner, and best known, perhaps, as the victim of Dryden's satire. He was a university man, and was intended for the ministry, but abandoned it on becoming a Catholic convert. Enjoyed the patronage of Charles I. and members of the nobility. The Revolution closed his dramatic career, and threw him for a time on the bounty of friends. He became a teacher, and finally died, in 1666, from exposure, in consequence of the Great Fire of London, which drove him from the city. Shirley has left us a larger number of plays than any other dramatist of this time, save Shakespeare, thirty-three in all, the greater part of which are romantic comedies. " The Traitor," " The Wedding," " The Young Admiral," and " The Royal Master," are some of his best-known plays. Shirley's characteristics as an author are :

(1) Fertility and originality.

(2) The condensation of his comedy interest into a single scene, which enabled it to be given separately, if desired, as a droll or farce.

(3) Ability to suit the tastes of his audience.

(4) His serious work superior to his lighter efforts.

(5) Numerous passages of poetic and picturesque beauty.

(6) Grossness of his works, yet an honest, moral purpose present. Vice never represented as enjoying an easy victory.

The minor dramatists of this period who contributed, each after his kind, to the dramatic literature, are not particularly noteworthy, and it will be sufficient, in consideration of our limited space, to enumerate them : RICHARD BROME, THOMAS RANDOLPH, WILLIAM CARTWRIGHT, JASPER MAYNE, THOMAS MAY, SIR JOHN SUCKLING, SHAKERLY MARMION, SIR JOHN DENHAM, WILLIAM HABINGTON, HENRY GLAPTHORNE, ROBERT TAILOR, LODOWICK BARRY, ROBERT DAVENPORT, LEWIS MACHIN, THOMAS RAWLINS, NATHANIEL RICHARDS, RICHARD LOVELACE, GEORGE RUGGLE, etc., etc.

One more illustrious name remains to be mentioned. JOHN MILTON was a man whose contributions to the drama were limited to three works, and one of these finds its sole home in the library. Nevertheless, by the greatness of these productions, aside from what he has in other fields of letters accomplished, he has enriched considerably the English literature, and also won for himself a worthy place amongst dramatists. It is not necessary to relate the life and deeds of this great epic poet. His energy, profound scholarship, honorable career, are too well known to demand more than mention here. In 1634 he produced the masques, "The Arcades" and "Comus," the latter of which stands unapproached in this realm of letters. It was at once the climax and the termination of the masque. Nothing worthy of the name ever followed it.

Milton was never connected directly with the drama of his day. He was a Puritan, and, though a liberal one, yet his life and manner of thought made such a connection impossible. Nevertheless, he is said to have made one hundred and two schemes of dramatic subjects on classic models ; sixty on scriptural topics, thirty-three on British history and five on Scottish history. He has left but one play, however, "Samson Agonistes" (1677).

This chronologically belongs to the time of the Restoration, but its spirit is Elizabethan. Both "Comus" and "Samson" reflect the moral indignation with which the representative of Puritanism regarded the social degradation. "Samson Agonistes" was never intended for the stage. There is no division into acts and scenes, and the catastrophe is announced by a messenger. A chorus is made use of. It is needless to speak of the great beauty of the poetry.

In the brief summary we have made we have glanced, we had not time for more, at the lives, works and literary peculiarities of the men whose names fill the brightest period of our literature, the Elizabethan. But a treatise on any age that looks only upon the great individuals who are its exponents must naturally be deficient. There is another view, a general one, which remains to be taken before our work approaches completion. In Shakespeare we have beheld the flower of this remarkable age. In his contemporaries and successors we perceive the seeds and observe the growth of the weed, corruption, that foretells decline. But we must not suppose a wide or stated interval to exist between the two. The flower and weed grew side by side. As the promising work of Greene, Peele and Marlowe was contemporaneous with Shakespeare's early endeavors, so was the hot-house plant of Beau-

mont and Fletcher's genius with his latei
ones.   Undoubtedly both Shakespeare and
Jonson exerted a wide influence on their fellows, but their successors were not as they
master-dramatists, and   imitative   seldom
reaches the   height   attained   by   original
genius.   With the growth of Puritanism the
popularity of the theatre naturally waned.
Supported by the Royalists alone its fortunes
fluctuated with those of its patrons, and its
manners reflected the manners of its patrons.
The early Elizabethan drama mirrors the
vigor, chivalry and manliness of the Elizabethan court.   The later period, belonging
to the reigns of James I. and Charles I. as
faithfully represent the effeminacy, immorality and corruption of those monarchs'
reigns.   The national life had ceased to be
great and offered no such powerful stimulus
to great efforts as did Elizabeth's England.
The stirring continental events, politics and
religion, were forbidden subjects to the dramatist.   Deprived of his choicest materials
and compelled to appeal to but half the public, it is not to be wondered at that the ideas
and sentiments of the play-wright became
warped and corrupted ; that he should accept and promulgate the doctrine of "divine

right of kings," that he should look leniently on the faults of his patrons and become infused with their loose morality. Exclusiveness, extravagance, coarseness, love of drinking, gaming and dress, were Royalistic characteristics of that time. These, as a result, permeate the drama. The luxuries and refinements of life grew more numerous. Fierceness abated and outward manners visibly improved, but secret vice and superstition prevailed to an astonishing extent.

The stage came to be restricted in various ways. Besides political and religious allusions being prohibited, the "jesting and profane" use of sacred names was forbidden ; no modern Christian king was permitted to be represented. Members of the nobility might no longer authorize plays in any part of the kingdom, nor companies remain more than fourteen days in any one place, excepting London. It is needless to say that most, if not all, of these restrictions, were repeatedly disregarded and the infringements were not always punished.

The hostility of the Puritans to the theatre was intense. Many of their objections were well founded, but ignorant of the fact that the English nature demands the existence of the drama, they desired not to reform and put to its best uses the stage, but to annihilate it. As long as the Court and nobility upheld it, this could not be done, but the desire found its expression in a strong anti-theatrical literature.

In 1625 " A Short Treatise of Stage Playes " was presented to the first Parliament of Charles I., requesting the closing of the theatres. Nothing was done, however, save to forbid Sunday performances. In 1632 Puritan enmity issued its most famous literary effort against the stage. " Histriomastix, the Players Scourge or Actors Tragedic," by William Prynne. This was the result of seven years' labor, and shows remarkable learning and enthusiasm. It is a book of more than a thousand closely printed pages, and attacks the stage at every point. Prynne condemns the theatre, the drama, the audiences, the players and especially assails a company in which women had for the first time taken part. Shortly before the appearance of the " Histriomastix " the Queen and her ladies had enacted a pastoral drama at Whitehall, and as the Court often composed the audience before which a favorite play was given, Prynne's attack involved the honor of the royal family as well as the drama.

The unfortunate author was summoned before the High Commission Court and Star Chamber. His book was condemned to be burnt and he to be expelled from the Bar and his Inn, to stand in the pillory, to lose both ears, to pay a fine of £5000 to the King, and to be perpetually imprisoned.

Prynne's punishment we cannot but regard as tyranical, and serving only to make him a martyr in the eyes of the Puritans. His book really had a good effect on the drama, as it served to check its excesses. In 1639–40 the serious political condition darkened the dramatic world as well. In 1641 the plague broke out, and temporarily closed the theatres. Christmas, 1641, saw but one play given at Court, and neither the King nor Queen was present at that. The Master of the Revels closes his register in June, 1642, with the entry of a play entitled " The Irish Rebellion," and " here," he adds, "ended my allowance of plays, for the war began in August, 1642." On the 2d of September the ordinance of the Lords and Commons commanded " that while these sad causes and set times of humiliation do continue, public

stage plays shall cease, and be forborne."
The theatres remained closed till the Restoration.

And so ends the half century containing the richest literary products and the most marvellous assembly of genius of our language. Few fields were left unexplored ; few types untried. Yet after Shakespeare's works nearly all is retrogressive. Jonson and Ford failed to reach the highest level in tragedy. Heywood does not uphold the Chronicle History. The numerous writers of tragi-comedy, that is the romantic tragedy, did not in that they lose sight of the highest moral ideals, attain the lasting success which they might have done.

The comedy alone progresses—progresses, but not improves. Throughout the works of Marston, Webster, Fletcher, Ford, Shirley and others, there is a sameness that makes these writers, despite their genius, wearisome to the ordinary reader. However various the themes and different the personality of the authors, this impression is not to be escaped. This is, no doubt, produced by the uniform lack of moderation displayed. All passions and emotions are depicted in excess, and the result on the reader is to produce indifference and fatigue. Yet we cannot disregard the sudden and delicate touches of Ford and Webster, Beaumont and Fletcher's pathos, Massinger's dignified sentiment and Shirley's poetical illustration, which lighten the otherwise monotonous li·erary vein.

It is in the verse that we find the most pronounced individuality of the prominent writers in the first part of this period. In the latter part this is less noticeable, for the lesser poets became careless and characterless in their writing as they were in their lives. Their prose also deserves mention as standing so entirely separate from the political, religious and oratorical prose of the time. This was due, of course, to obvious reasons. The stage had to do with conversation not dissertations. One thing more must not be forgotten, the inter-dependence of the Elizabethan poets. Not alone, but as influencing and being influenced by one another, must they be studied for an impartial judgment of their achievements and worth.

V.

FROM THE RESTORATION TO THE CLOSE OF THE EIGHTEENTH CENTURY (1660–1800).

ALTHOUGH the theatres in England were closed by act of Parliament in August, 1642, and had fallen into disrepute and met with neglect before this, such was the vitality of the drama that it never wholly ceased to be represented, but in one form or another bridged over the period of the Protectorate and survived all opposition. In defiance of ordinances, performances were given clandestinely, particularly at the homes of the royalist nobility, and sometimes they were given openly, when they were suppressed by the means of the soldiery.

Though plays were forbidden to be performed, there was no law to prevent their being published. In consequence of this not only were the plays of the Elizabethan dramatists printed and widely read, but likewise works of contemporaneous writers, such as FRANCIS QUARLES, SIR ASTON COKAIN, SIR

WILLIAM DAVENANT, WILLIAM CHAMBERLAYNE, and THOMAS KILLIGREW, were scattered throughout royalistic England. Naturally politics and religion became topics for discussion with an invariable hostility to Puritanism and the Commonwealth.

It was at this time that an actor, by name Robert Cox, in his ingenious attempts to defeat the object of the law, and to maintain himself by means of his old calling, evolved what were then termed *drolls*, and which later came to be called *farces.* They were dialogues and comic scenes taken from well-known plays. Passing under another name, these fragments were usually permitted to be given without molestation or interference.

The drama fostered in this its darkest hour in England by the infrequent performances of *drolls*, by *sub rosa* entertainments, by its literature and by a strong friendly feeling in the large royalistic population, found a champion in SIR WILLIAM DAVENANT (1605–1668). This irrepressible nobleman and play-wright forms the connecting link between the Elizabethan and the Restoration drama. Belonging, as he does, to the reigns of three of the Stuarts, he was poet-laureate under Charles I., without originality or great genius, but

indomitable and energetic, he may be said to
be a fit exponent of the play of his day, which
was kept alive only by the energy and perseverance of such men as himself. In 1656
Davenant, by a clever application, backed by
an equally clever argument, was granted the
privilege of giving an entertainment, to con-
sist of declamation and music, "after the
manner of the ancients," at Rutland House, in
Aldersgate Street. The opera, "The Siege of
Rhodes," described by Davenant as "a
Representation by the Art of Prospective in
Scenes, and the story sung," followed shortly
the first entertainment. Then came the
operas, "The History of Sir Francis Drake"
and "The Cruelty of the Spaniards in Peru."
Lastly Davenant ventured boldly to produce
regular plays, and he was not interfered with.
Thus painting and music befriended and
restored the drama, only afterwards, however,
to assail and weaken it. For the way was
opened for that formidable rival of the play,
the opera, and accessories were introduced,
which contributed largely to its degeneracy,
music and scenery.

The return of Charles II. to his throne in
1660 was the signal for the re-opening of the
theatres, although several had anticipated

that event and were already in existence on his arrival. Two leading companies were soon in receipt of royal patents. The first was called " The Duke of York's Servants," and was under the management of Davenant ; the second was " The King's Servants," commonly called the "Old Actors," and was headed by Killigrew, a name long and honorably connected with the stage. Davenant's theatre was at Lincoln's Inn Fields after 1662, Killigrew's from 1663 near Drury Lane, and was named the Theatre Royal. With the Restoration the stage entered upon a career of renewed popularity and unprecedented favor. The theatres were improved and women instead of boys assumed without resistance the female parts. Actors and dramatists were eagerly sought out and lionized by the Court and society. Nell Gwynn and the tragedian Betterton were favorites at that time.

But though stamped with the favor of king and people, surrounded and equipped as it had never been before, its actors courted and its writers lauded, yet the drama degenerated. In the fifty years succeeding the Restoration we have but two tragedians worthy of being ranked even with the secondary lights of the

Elizabethan period, Dryden and Otway. The literary sins of the former, and the short life of the latter, have left us unfortunately but little even here to be admired and perpetuated. Bare as were the Stuart reigns of glorious deeds, unfortunate as their arms had been in the field, clouded by disgrace as they so frequently were, it is not strange that tragedy should decline in merit and favor amongst their play-writers. Having been exiled and deprived of national existence for a period, and during that time becoming infected with the gayety and brilliancy of France, the English Court, on its reassembling, wished to contemplate an amusing and flattering reflection rather than a sombre, instructive and perhaps detracting one. Too long depressed and corrupted by foreign influences, the Court encouraged in life and on the stage a frivolity, superficiality, gayety, lewdness and freedom from all restraint, that has made the time and literature of Charles II. England's disgrace. But it must be remembered in dwelling upon this period that these words of reproach concern only the Court and the theatre, and do not apply to the great mass of the people who looked with indignation upon the existing corruption in metropolitan circles, and whom the stage either misrepresents or does not represent at all.

The result of the depraved taste of its patrons on the drama was to make it equally depraved, and to bring forth a coterie of dramatists who, for brilliancy of dialogue, for wit, humor and construction, have rarely, and for obscenity and immorality, certainly never been equaled. With these men virtue is but a name, which serves as a cloak to hide the most revolting sins. Vice exists only in those who are discovered. Nothing is reprehensible save exposure. Stupidity, not wickedness, is condemned. Marriage is not a sacred rite but a convenience, and an inevitable forerunner of crime.

This state of things could not, of course, exist long. Being contrary to the English nature it must perish. A reaction was inevitable. A reaction that would temporarily paralyze while purifying the drama. With the accession of William and Mary in 1688, this reaction began. The Court frowned upon the indecencies of the theatre. In 1704 Anne issued a royal order against its improprieties. A national war broke down the distinctions between Royalist and Puritan, and the stage ceased to reflect one phase of life alone. Finally, with Addison's " Cato," in 1713, and Steele's comedies, a crusade was made against the imperfections, real and imagined, of the stage.

With the very best of intentions these writers brought about the most disastrous results. For nearly a hundred years after the production of " Cato " no really great tragedy was written. The attempt to introduce pseudo-classicism failed, but this imitation of foreign models, stamped with the approval of the day, diverted serious drama from its natural course. The immediate result was the translation and adaptation of the French, and an inferior imitation of an inferior school. This did not satisfy, and finally we evolve the domestic tragedy, the sentimental drama, which has all the desired morality of tone, and more than enough of morality of dialogue. Comedy in the Restoration lost its vigor and poetry, with Steele its viciousness and superficial brilliancy. Very little being left, a leavening of sentiment was introduced to make it acceptable. Both the serious and comic drama sank into mediocrity and imitation of French and Spanish models. Little of real value was written.

Into this field of sloth and unworthiness David Garrick came, who, by his genius and industry, was first to shame, then rouse his countrymen. His unceasing efforts in reviving the Elizabethan and Restoration dramatists, revealed to his age what had been done in the drama in the past, and, by his innumerable bright farces, and the comedies of the elder Colman and himself, showed what might be done in the future. Quickly follow the works of Sheridan, Goldsmith, the younger Colman, O'Keefe, etc., and the comedy of the latter half of the eighteenth century may justly be said to rival that of the Restoration in brilliancy, and excel it in purity and tone.

I do not think this period has ever received its just meed of praise. A period that has produced such sterling works as " The Rivals," " School for Scandal," " Heir at Law," " She Stoops to Conquer," " Wild Oats," is worthy of more attention than it has received.

The domestic drama likewise has advanced, and though still full of imperfections, has developed into the poetic and interesting, if unnatural, melodrama, such as " The Iron Chest." Tragedy has contributed " Douglas," " The Roman Father," " Virginia," etc., none, however, of great merit.

At the close of the eighteenth century we
find the stage in possession of a brilliant
comedy, an entertaining melodrama, a mediocre tragedy, an amusing farce, and an infant
and popular opera.

Having rapidly glanced at the progress of
the English drama during the one hundred
and forty years which this lecture covers, we
must now turn our attention to the steps by
which this progress was made. We have
already stated that Davenant's musical pieces,
or operas, as "The Siege of Rhodes," had
opened the way for the return of the drama
proper ; that the drama of this epoch, taking
its initiative from the Court which supported
it, was not a national development, but a
product of the combined influence of the
classic, the French, the Italian and the Spanish
play, reflecting brilliantly in its tragedy an
unreal existence, and in its comedy the
depraved Court of the second Charles ; that
the popularity of the stage and its occu-
pants were equaled only by their immorality.

Although we have assigned already reasons
for the condition of the Restoration drama,
yet we have not accounted for the inferior
English product based on such French

classics as Molière and Racine. It is remarkable that a series of French writers, possessing so many excellencies, should, by their influence, produce a series of English writers possessing so many faults. To be sure the French models chosen in tragedy, Corneille and Racine, were pseudo - classicists and exponents of an unnatural school, and in so far their direct effect was injurious. But these writers were in perfect sympathy with their national spirit and time, and possess many excellencies. It is unfortunate that the English failed to perceive this important lesson of sympathy with one's people and age, and neglecting the good points, should have copied only the meretricious. The spirit of French tragedy is entirely foreign to the English nature, and neither that nor its sound morality was caught by the British writer. To Racine and Corneille English tragedy became indebted for its form and verse, for the substitution of rime for blank verse ; but its spirit was derived from the wildly improbable French romances of Mlle. de Scudery, etc., which are filled with astonishing heroic deeds, melodious names, ravishing descriptions, undying love ; heroes like Artamanes, who alone slay one hundred thousand men ;

heroines who suffer unspeakable sorrows ; villains of incomparable wickedness.

Molière, the model taken for comedy, must not be held accountable for the sins of his British‚ imitators.   He was apparently entirely above and beyond the comprehension of his island neighbors.   Fortunately for comedy, it was deemed unsuitable for rime, and passed almost wholly into prose.   Even in tragedy the innovation or rather revival (for it had previously existed) of rime being artificial, could not live long.   Dryden's whim gave it a passing success, as his support did the " heroic " tragedy, both of which were doomed when his approbation should be withdrawn.

The Italian influence is confined chiefly to the introduction of the opera and of music as an accessory to the play.   Shakespeare's and Fletcher's plays become adorned with musical accompaniments.   Dryden, Gay and later Sheridan produced operas.   Finally the ballet was introduced.   All of these novelties, however good in themselves, were evil in their effects, in so far as they individually and collectively detracted from the demands on the literary element in the play.   Yet to the credit of the English people be it said that

even in that age of false and perverted taste
a sufficient admiration for the Elizabethan
dramas existed to warrant their production,
though unfortunately adapted, re-arranged
and generally tortured.

The attempt to re-establish the use of
rime in English tragedy was first made by
Robert Boyle, Earl of Orrery (–1679). He
was the originator of that dramatic type of
doubtful value, the " heroic " drama. The
first of these remarkable productions was his
" Black Prince," which was acted in 1667.
This was followed by a number of others, all
equally uninteresting, unnatural and unreal.
They are to be noted only for the consistency
with which the " heroic " couplet is used.

The champion of the " heroic " dráma, however, the man whose genius alone made it
popular and whose example gave it whatever
lease of life it had, was that inconsistent literary dictator of his age, JOHN DRYDEN (1631–
1700). This intellectual giant, whose energies were so misdirected, whose self-conceit
was so vast, whose opportunities for good
were so great, and whose attainments in this
direction were so insignificant, was the central figure of the Restoration literature. One
·of the greatest masters of style and verse in

our language, the greatest poet of his time, undoubtedly he was the man and the only man who might have turned the current of corruption into purer channels and have revived the Elizabethan spirit of the drama. But the man was not so great as the poet, and Dryden espoused the cause of that vitiated taste which sought entertainment in the "heroic" drama and the licentious comedy. Although thoroughly disliking the latter dramatic type, and believing himself unsuited for its requirements, yet, freed as he was here from false notions of verse (comedy was now written in prose) some of his most brilliant achievements were in this field.

Dryden was a well-known writer and a member of the Royal Society before he became associated with the stage. Necessity first induced him to seek this means of earning a livelihood. His earliest works were not successful. In conjunction with his brother-in-law, Sir Robert Howard, he produced "The Indian Queen," in 1664, which met with considerable favor. In the following year, 1665, Dryden's tragedy, "The Indian Emperor, or The Conquest of Mexico by the Spaniards," was received with enthusiastic applause. Both of these plays were specimens of the "heroic"·

drama.   Love and honor were the all absorb-
ing subjects.   The riming couplet was used
throughout and at once attained popularity.
Dryden entered immediately the front rank
of contemporary dramatists, and in his own
estimation, of all dramatists.

In 1667 or 68 Dryden published his " Essay
of Dramatic Poesy."   This excellent treatise
contains many truths and a large number of
sophisms.   Dryden recognizes the exalted
position of the English stage, refutes many
erroneous accusations made against it, and
perceives many of the merits in Shakespeare
and Fletcher.   But by this article he also endeavors to justify the substitution of rime for
blank verse.   His defence of rime may be
rejected unhesitatingly.   Indeed in later years
he did not scruple when weary of rime to
discard it and to return to blank verse.

About 1679 he published a second essay
on the subject, entitled "Grounds of Criticism in Tragedy," in which his views are
seen to be greatly altered, and by which
he dooms the "heroic" tragedy.   He perceives the errors of extravagance and over-
elaboration, and begins to desire those
powers of compactness and characterization
so admirably displayed by Shakespeare.   It

is unfortunate that his admiration of the great poet should have led him to mutilate his works. His adaptation of " The Tempest," for which Davenant is partly responsible, was an early attempt, it is true. But " Troilus and Cressida, or Truth Found Too Late," and "All for Love, or The World Well Lost " (Shakespeare's " Antony and Cleopatra "), were later works. The lastnamed is not unworthy of praise, as it contains many beautiful passages and shows what Dryden's genius, rightly directed, might have accomplished. In his declining years the poet acknowledges his mistake and his sin against literature in a pathetic " Ode to Mrs. Anne Killigrew " (1686).

His best known plays that have not been mentioned already, are " Secret Love, or The Maiden Queen " (1667), " Tyrranic Love, or The Royal Martyr" (1669), " Almanzor and Almahide, or The Conquest of Granada by the Spaniards" (1670), " Don Sebastian " (1690), " King Arthur " (1691), " The Spanish Friar " (1681), " Sir Martin Mar-All " (1667), " Marriage-a-la-Mode " (1673), etc., etc.

Besides Dryden, the drama of the Restoration, that is to say, the drama which extends from 1660 to the production of Addison's

"Cato" in 1713, boasts the names of such writers of tragedy as ELKANAH SETTLE, JOHN CROWNE, NATHANIEL LEE, THOMAS OTWAY, THOMAS SOUTHERNE, GEORGE GRANVILLE, LORD LANSDOWNE, and NICHOLAS ROWE; and of such writers of comedy as SIR GEORGE ETHEREGE, SIR GEORGE SEDLEY, JOHN LACY, MRS. APHRO BEHN, MRS. CENTLIVRE, MRS. MANLEY, THOMAS D'URFEY, THOMAS SHADWELL, WILLIAM WYCHERLY, SIR JOHN VANBURGH, GEORGE FARQUHAR, WILLIAM CONGREVE and COLLEY CIBBER. By this somewhat arbitrary division into writers of tragedies and writers of comedy, it is not intended to imply that the dramatists whose names have been placed in the one list never wrote anything outside of the class in which they occur. But it is intended to show in what class their best work, and the greater part of it, has been done; the work by which they earned their fame and which entitles them to remembrance.

JOHN CROWNE (˙ –1703 circ.) was a dramatist who knew what pleased his audience and gave it to them. As a result he was a popular but not an excellent author. He wrote both in rime and blank verse, though he handled the latter better. His successful compositions include both tragedies and

comedies.   Possessed of considerable skill
and fluency, he lacks refinement and accuracy.
His tragedies include "The Destruction of
Jerusalem," "Thyestes" and "Regulus."
Amongst his comedies may be noted "Sir
Courtley Nice," "City Politicks" and "Mar-
ried Beau."

NATHANIEL LEE (1650-1690), a successful
writer of this period, was a man of considerable power, impetuous, ambitious, passionate ;
so miserably excitable of temperament that
in 1684 he was for some time insane, and in
1690 met his death—it is said in a drunken
fit.   He composed in rime and belonged to
Dryden's "heroic" school until 1677, when
he began to use blank verse.   His plays, of
which the best known are "The Rival
Queens" (1677), and "The Massacre of Paris"
(1690), are extravagant and bombastic.

THOMAS OTWAY (1651-1685) is a lamentable
instance of a man possessed of great genius,
but whose brilliant faculties have been
blunted and prematurely destroyed by weakness and immorality ; a man whose grave
was dug early by despair and debauchery.
It is true that he was unfortunate.   He had
been well educated, but was left penniless.
It was his misfortune to love without recipro-

cation. He was at times favored, at times
rebuffed by noble patrons. His life was one
of recklessness and wretchedness. His work
reflects this. Sometimes it is coarse and
repellent, oftener inexpressibly tender and
beautiful. He excels in his love scenes.
Notwithstanding all his faults he has written
probably the finest tragedy in the Restoration
drama, " Venice Preserved." The subject of
this play, a conspiracy to overthrow the
Venetian oligarchic despotism, is admirably
chosen, being both interesting and dramatic.
The characters of Belvidera, the heroine
who induces her husband to betray the conspiracy, Jaffier, the traitor, and Pierre, the
patriot, are excellently drawn, and have
served to maintain the popularity of the
piece even into recent times. Other of
Otway's plays are " Don Carlos," " The
Orphan," " Caius Marius " (a willful plagiar-
ism), " The Atheist," etc. His comedies are
wretched compositions.

THOMAS SOUTHERNE (1660–1746) was a
prominent and respected author of his time.
" Oroonoko " (1696), " The Fatal Marriage "
(1694), and " The Loyal Brother " are amongst
his contributions to the drama.

GEORGE GRANVILLE, LORD LANSDOWNE

(1667–1733), is chiefly interesting in that his work, " Heroic Love," may be said to connect the Restoration and "Augustan" period. Of no particular merit as an author.

NICHOLAS ROWE (1673–1718) was in his time dramatist, poet-laureate and editor of Shakespeare's plays. His fame rests chiefly upon this last undertaking. Notwithstanding his admiration of Shakespeare and his desire to follow in his foot-steps, Rowe showed himself unable to appreciate his master when he said that Shakespeare excelled in male characters only. As a dramatist Rowe was gifted with refinement, power and considerable skill in portraying character and in devising situations. He was lacking, however, in poetic passion and elevation. " Jane Shore " (1714), "Lady Jane Grey (1715), and " The Royal Convert " (1707), are his most notable works, the first of which is still occasionally acted.

SIR GEORGE ETHEREGE (1636–1694 circ.), the first in point of time on our list of comic dramatists, contributed three plays to the stage of the later Stuarts, " The Comical Revenge, or Love in a Tub," " She Would if She Could," and " The Man of Mode, or Sir Topling Flutter. Where there is so little to commend it is just as well to be silent, a remark which is equally applicable to the productions of Sir George Sedley and Thomas D'Urfey, a plagiarist of the deepest die.

John Lacy (died 1681) was one of those actors who fought under the Stuart banner during the Revolution, and who in 1660 returned with Charles to re-pursue his former avocation of player, to which was subsequently added that of play-wright. Though coarse, there is much brightness and skill shown in his comedies, the best of which is "The Old Troop." It is to this actor-author that we owe that marvelous adaptation of Shakespeare's "Taming of the Shrew," "Sauny the Scot."

Mrs. Aphro Behn, (the divine Astræa) Mrs. Manly and Mrs. Centlivre, form a trio of female dramatists whose plays were many and revolting. In the mass of disreputable matter which these women wrote, but two comedies (both Mrs. Centlivre's) deserve any praise. "The Busy Body," and "The Wonder a Woman Keeps a Secret." The former contains the excellent character of Marplot, and the latter that of Don Felix.

Thomas Shadwell (1640–1692), poet-

laureate and royal historiographer to William and Mary, was a writer who, though
coarse, was evidently an opponent of social
wrongs. He admired Ben Jonson and sought
to imitate him.   In his life and temperament
he resembled his master, though falling short
in merit.   A list of his plays includes " The
Sullen Lovers, or The Impertinents," " The
Virtuoso," " Epsom Wells," " The Lancashire
Witches."   Shadwell is one of the first writers
to introduce the character of an Irishman
into comedy.

Despite the ascendency the " heroic "
drama had attained under Dryden, there
were many who were not blind to its defects
and lamented its influence. Accordingly, to
counteract the effect of this pernicious type,
and to purify the public taste, the riming
tragedies were attacked by that most powerful of weapons, ridicule. In 1671 appeared
the famous burlesque-comedy, " The Rehearsal," written by George Villiers, Duke of
Buckingham, and others. This play was the
result of much and prolonged labor, which
was rewarded by unprecedented success.
Twenty-one editions were published, and
many imitations of it have appeared in subsequent years, the most noteworthy being

Sheridan's "Critic." Its effect on the "heroic" type must have been considerable, though so long as Dryden wrote not even ridicule could destroy its popularity. Yet without the check imposed by "The Rehearsal," it is difficult to say to what extremes the "heroic" drama might not have gone.

We now approach that quartette of comedians whose brilliancy and immorality have attracted the admiration and disgust of all succeeding generations. WYCHERLY (who in point of time preceded the others, and might rather be said to be a contemporary of DRYDEN), CONGREVE, VANBURGH and FARQUHAR. The first, whose broad and pointed wit was once so popular, but is to us so unnatural, was the model for the three younger men. They were more gifted, more decent and more refined than Wycherly, though equally as corrupt. Of the four, Congreve has been given the first place by reason of his surpassing brilliancy of dialogue, wit and humor. After a long interval this school was to reappear in a purified but equally meritorious form in Sheridan and Colman, in whom it was to reach its climax and culmination.

WILLIAM WYCHERLY (1640–1715), a vicious but remarkably powerful comic dramatist, is

in his dramas and his life a fit exponent of
the corrupt and superficial Court of Charles
II.   In his plays we meet with strong
characters, acting and speaking naturally—
we might almost say too much so.   His satire
is keen and his wit cynical and merciless.
He uncloaks vice, it is true, but less with a
purpose of rendering punishment than of
furnishing amusement.   " Love in a Wood "
(1672), " The Dancing Master (1673), " The
Country Wife " (1675), and " The Plain
Dealer " (1677), are his best known works.
" The Country Wife," as Wycherly wrote it,
is an appalling and vicious picture of a certain
phase of Restoration life.   Remodeled by
Garrick, as " The Country Girl," in which
the spirit and cynicism is preserved, while
much that is offensive has been eliminated, it
has been successfully revived at various times.
The favor with which it has met being largely
due to the character of Peggy, a hoyden,
which, in the hands of a clever actress, may
be made a delightful role.   The character
won fame at different times and in different
lands for two charming actresses, Mrs. Jordan
and Ada Rehan.   " The Plain Dealer " is an
English version of Molière's " Misanthrope."
Wycherley's play is far inferior to the French

model, and his hero, "Manly," is an example of now little Molière was understood by his would-be British followers. Although a disgusting, it is undoubtedly a powerful play. "The Dancing Master," composed on a Spanish model, is exceedingly clever and interesting.

WILLIAM CONGREVE (1670–1729) was the brightest luminary of the later Restoration drama. Dryden, in his old age, perceiving the merit of the young author, gladly yielded his exalted position to the only man whom he deemed worthy to be his successor. It was perhaps unfortunate that Congreve's genius was so universally recognized in his own day. Had it been otherwise he might have been spurred on to greater endeavors.

As it was he has left but five works, one of which, "The Mourning Bride" (1697), is a tragedy. His first production, "The Old Bachelor" (1693), an excellent though not a strikingly original work, met with unstinted applause. "The Double Dealer," produced the same year, is a comedy of the first rank, and won enthusiastic praise from its author's contemporaries. Two unusually strong characters found in this piece are Maskwell and Lady Touchwood. "Love for Love" appeared in 1695, "The Way of the World" in 1700. The latter, though of great excellence, failed in representation. After this Congreve abandoned play-writing. His single tragedy, "The Mourning Bride" (1697) reveals the one-sidedness of Congreve's art. He was not a tragedian. He was also the author of a masque, "The Judgement of Paris," and of an opera, "Semele," neither of much importance.   .

His dramatic achievements, though bringing him great fame, were not the source of the same pride to Congreve that they would have been to another man. He preferred the title of an English gentleman to that of a dramatist. Nevertheless it is as dramatist that he will be remembered longest. In the brilliancy, grace and ease of his dialogue he excelled all contemporaries and most predecessors. He was one of the wittiest of Englishmen and his plays are amongst the wittiest in the drama. His characters and plots are vigorously and skillfully handled. But unfortunately Congreve's merits as a writer are only superficial ones. The spirit of his works, as well as their language, is frivolous and immoral.

SIR JOHN VANBURGH (1666 circ.–1726), as

well as being one of the leading dramatists
was also one of the most eminent architects
of his day. His comedies are vivacious,
fluent, well-constructed and sparkling. One
of his characters is strikingly original and life-
like, Lord Foppington in "The Relapse, or
Virtue in Danger." This play, produced in
1697, was Vanburgh's first and best work.
"The Provoked Wife," "The Confederacy,"
"The Mistake," "The False Friend," and an
unfinished play, which Cibber afterwards
completed and presented in 1728 under the
title of "The Provoked Husband," (Vanbrugh
had named it "A Trip to London"), all show
their author in a highly brilliant but immoral
light.

GEORGE FARQUHAR (1678–1707) was one of
the first of the distinguished Irishmen who
have written for the stage, a list of whose
names includes Sheridan, Goldsmith, Boucicault, etc., etc. Possessed of those qualities
which were shared in general by his contemporaries, brilliancy, vivacity, humor, accuracy in description of a certain kind of manners, coarseness and invention, Farquhar also
revealed more freshness and originality than
did his colleagues. His characters and situations are often dubious, but his treatment of

them is vigorous and interesting. His masterpiece is " The Beaux' Stratagem " (1707), which has ever been a favorite on the stage, and which contains one of Garrick's best roles, Archer. " The Recruiting Officer " is another highly successful effort. " The Inconstant " (1703), suggested by Fletcher's " Wild Goose Chase," is likewise a very meritorious work. His first play, " Love in a Bottle," was given to the public which received it with approbation, in 1698.

COLLEY CIBBER (1671–1757) was an actor, author and manager. He was a great favorite as an actor, particularly in the role of fops, and was seen on the stage as late as 1745, although he retired in 1732. In 1730 he was appointed poet laureate. As a author he endeavored, though not always successfully, to reform the comedy of his day. " Love's Last Shift," suggested by Vanbrugh's " The Relapse," " Woman's Wit," " The Careless Husband," The Lady's Last Stake," and " She Would and She Would Not," are commendable efforts. The last-named is still occasionally given, and constitutes one of the bills in Mr. Augustin Daly's extensive repertoire.

We have now reached an important epoch in the history of the drama. From the earliest times we have watched it acquire growth, vigor, form, symm y. The inner ethical beauties and the   ward charms of verse and dialogue have been ,elaborated. In Shakespeare we have beheld the apex of dramatic perfectic , In his immediate successors, the Elizabethan dramatists, we have noticed the decl', ,;of ethical perception, in symmetry and gr.,dually in vigor and verse. Then came the Civil War, a period barely bridged by the supporters of the drama. With the accession of Charles the drama sprang once more into life, but though not wanting in talented authors to support it, it was so hampered, restrained and corrupted by false notions of life, manners and poetry that all gund qualities, save brilliancy and fluency, we discarded, and its baser qualities, its imperfe ons were glaringly exhibited. The drama without a moral purpose can not exist long. "When play-writing sinks to the level it did in the Restoration authors, it must either be annihilated or purified. The most forcible and almost irrefutable attack the stage ever received was made at this period (1698) by the famous JEREMY COLLIER, in his book, "A Short View of the Immorality and Profaneness of the English Stage." Dryden,

Congreve and Vanbrugh all attempted to refute, but really maintained Collier's assertions. The effect made by this book was extensive and visible. It became popular to save the sinners in the fifth act. Colly Cibber made earnest efforts for improvements. But the reformation, and well-nigh the annihilation, of the drama was brought about by those masters of style, and eminently well-intentioned men, Addison and Steele. It is unquestionably to these authors that we owe the purification of the stage. It is unfortunate that we must ascribe also to one of them the death, or at least the prolonged sleep, of English tragedy. Comedy, being a description of manners and characters, is more tenacious of life than her serious sister, and will always have a past, a present and a future. Tragedy, like a camelia, is a flower demanding certain conditions of growth, deprived of which it withers and perishes.

It is seldom that it is granted to a man to achieve lasting fame by a single work. Yet upon JOSEPH ADDISON (1672–1719) was bestowed this favor. "Cato," a tragedy on classical models, or what Addison took to be classical models, was the work that established its author's fame as a dramatist, and marks an epoch in dramatic history. Built on the plan it is, the play is unnatural in action, not happy in its characterization and contains a number of intrusive episodes. Its dialogue, though often stilted, is chaste and sometimes effective. Its extraordinary success was due entirely to the time in which it was produced, when hostile politicians eagerly sought and approved what they chose to consider as in accordance and praise of their deeds and views. "Cato" was not intended for the stage, and was not produced until 1713, many years after it was first written. The injury it did to tragedy was not in the adoption of a purer tone, but in the discarding of the natural demands and form of English drama, and the apparently successful introduction of rules foreign to its existence.

SIR RICHARD STEELE (1671–1729) seconded Addison in his endeavor to correct the manners and morals of that period, and together they may be said to have in a large measure succeeded. Certain it is that licentiousness and indecency were henceforth banished from the stage. Steele exercised his talents to popularizing virtue and to rendering profanity and immorality abhorrent: But lacking Shakespearean vigor and the Restoration brilliancy, and discarding its broad wit and coarse intrigue, Steele was obliged to call into use sentiment to make his plays acceptable. This was the origin of the " sentimental " comedy, which, with the " sentimental " drama, both inferior dramatic types, held the stage for many years. Steele's best plays are " The Funeral or Grief à la Mode " (1702) (an excellent work), " The Lying Lover " (the first instance of "sentimental" comedy proper), " The Tender Husband (1705), and " The Conscious Lovers " (1722).

The Restoration drama may be said to cease with the death of Anne, though it had practically disappeared with the advent of Steele and Addison some years before. A few plays belonging to the old school appeared afterwards, Cibber's version of Vanbrugh's " A Provoked Husband," in 1729, being the last of these. With this solitary exception we may say that from 1714 to the production of the elder Colman's " Jealous Wife," in 1761, or for a period of nearly fifty years, no genuinely meritorious comedy was produced. As regards original productions, the stage was given up to mediocre tragedies, which were soon forgotten, opera, domestic tragedy, or melodrama, sentimental comedy and farce.

The tragedies of this period do not call for notice.

The operas in that they were so unusually popular, especially one of them, must not be passed by. Ever since Davenant's "Siege of Rhodes," produced during the Commonwealth, this style of performance had been growing in favor. Music had been written to many plays; dances and songs had been introduced. Italian opera in one form or another had become an institution. In 1727 GAY's famous "Beggar's Opera" appeared. Its success was so great that it was given in · London for sixty-three consecutive nights, a run then unprecedented, and met with equal applause in the provinces. For the time being Italian opera was driven from London. Such was the rage his work created that ladies carried about fans with the songs written on them, the leading singer married a duke, and John Gay, dying in 1732, was buried in Westminster Abbey.

Amongst the farce writers of this period, a class in which we find the names of Garrick and Fielding, must be mentioned one of the most remarkable figures in the history of the drama, SAMUEL FOOTE : a university man, a law student, a man who squandered three fortunes, an actor, an author of some twenty-five elongated farces, a manager, who for ten years successfully kept his theatre, the Haymarket, open without license. His most popular pieces were "The Diversions of a Morning," his initial effort, "The Auction of Pictures," " The Mirror," in which the Methodists are satirized, "The Bankrupt," which attacks the newspapers, "The Liar," etc. He died in 1777.

HENRY FIELDING (1707–1754) wrote some twenty pieces, of which the best known are " The Wedding Day " and " Tom Thumb."

DAVID GARRICK (1716–1779) is one of the most illustrious names in the annals of the stage or the history of the drama. It will pass without question, I take it, that Garrick was one of the greatest actors the English stage has ever seen. His achievements in this line are too well known for mention here. The actor who was equally great as tragedian or comedian, will not soon be forgotten. What he did for the drama as an author was probably not considerable, although he wrote some of the best farces of his century, and assisted in the composition of one of the best comedies of his time. It is, however, by his untiring and successful efforts to re-instate the Elizabethan drama, and especially Shakespeare, in the possession of the stage, and the favor of the critics and people, that he has won for himself unending praise.

Garrick perceived the low ebb to which the drama had sunk. He perceived the neglect for the masters, and the vitiated taste of the people, who could applaud such works as " The Beggar's Opera," and " George Barnwell." Early inspired with a love for the theatre and what was best in it, he was repelled by the roaring cant that passed for tragedy, the whining grief, the unreal terror and love-making then common to the stage. In 1740 the young ambitious Garrick determined to revive Shakespeare and reform the theatre. He made his first appearance as an actor under the name of Lyddal at Ipswich, assuming the character of " Aboan " in Southerne's "Oroonoko." He was so favorably received that he shortly risked a London debut as Richard III. This took place at Goodman's Fields, and was a tremendous success. Garrick's salary at this time was £5 a week. From this time on his success was assured. In 1747 Garrick became manager of the

Drury Lane Theatre, which position he retained until 1776. During his management
he produced in the orignal texts twenty-four
of Shakespeare's works.

He revived a number of the Restoration
plays, after having made suitable alterations
and eliminations. Amongst these plays may
be named " The Rehearsal," " Country Wife,"
(called by Garrick " The Country Girl,")
" The Mistake," " The Wonder," " Mourning
Bride," " Venice Preserved," etc. Of the
Elizabethans, Shakespeare, Jonson and
Fletcher were the favored authors. He produced of the contemporaneous drama Dr.
Johnson's " Irene," which failed as a stage representation; Younge's tragedies, " The Brothers " (1719), and " The Revenge " (1721),
(neither of much lasting merit, though sufficiently successful to yield Younge a profit of
£1,000, which he gave to the missionaries):
Edward Moore's " Gamester " (1753); Glover's
" Boadicea "; Whitehead's tragedies, " The
Roman Father " (1750) and " Creusa " (1754);
both highly praised in their day ; Dr. Smol-
lett's " Reprisal," a farce ; Home's " Douglas "; Crisp's " Virginia "; Colman's " Polly
Honeycombe " and " The Jealous Wife," etc.,
also his own numerous farces and his joint

comedy with Colman, " The Clandestine Marriage."

For twenty-nine years his theatre was the home of all that was worthiest in the native English Drama. He revived the best of former ages, and encouraged the best of his own. He was not always wise in his handling of Shakespeare's works, as we view them to-day, but he was " wise in his generation." In 1769 he arranged a Shakespeare Jubilee at Stratford-upon-Avon, and afterwards represented it at Drury Lane for ninety-two successive nights.

A list of his own works would include " The Clandestine Marriage," " Bon Ton," " The Irish Widow," " Lilliput," " Lethe," "Farmer's Return from London," " The Guardian," etc., etc.

He retired from management in 1776 ; made his final appearance as " Don Felix," in Mrs. Centlivre's " The Wonder," June 10th, 1776 ; died January 20th, 1779, and was buried in Westminster Abbey. David Garrick, a good husband, a polished gentleman, a great actor, he was the ornament of his age, and the reformer of the stage and dramatic literature. He found the theatre at its lowest ebb and he resigned it elevated and re- invigorated into the hands of a series of brilliant writers. Garrick wished to make the theatre a place of learning and culture. So far did he succeed that it has been said there were in his day four estates, the King, Lords, Commons and the Drury Lane Theatre.

A name intimately associated with David Garrick's is that of GEORGE COLMAN, the elder (1732–1794). A writer of considerable merit of farces and comedies, such as " Polly Honeycombe " (1760), "The Jealous Wife " (1761), and " The Clandestine Marriage " (1766). Colman was also, for some time, joint manager of Convent Garden, and for many years manager of the Haymarket Theatre. While at Convent Garden, Colman produced plays by Isaac Bickerstaafe, Arthur Murphy, Mrs. Inchbald, etc., and during his managerial career Goldsmith's " She Stoops to Conquer," O'Keefe's works and those of his son. His own plays were strong in character, and were aimed at fashionable follies.

The dramatists of the latter half of the eighteenth century are obscured by the radiance emanating from one great name, a name that belongs alike to a statesman, an orator and a dramatist, RICHARD BRINSLEY SHERIDAN. Richard Brinsley (1751–1816)

was the son of an Irish actor, Thomas Sheridan, and a famous novelist, Frances Sheridan.
He was born in Dublin, and was well
educated. Early in life he eloped with,
secretly married, and fought two duels for a
beautiful singer, by name Linley.

On the 17th of January, 1775, his comedy,
" The Rivals," was produced at Convent Garden. Owing to the bad rendering of Sir
Lucius O'Trigger by the actor who assumed
that part, the play failed on the first night ;
but a change being made in the cast, the
comedy became the great favorite it has remained ever since.

In conjunction with his father-in-law and
Dr. Ford, Sheridan bought Garrick's interest
in Drury Lane in the year 1776.

In 1777 appeared " The School for Scandal,"
which has been termed the best comedy in
the English language. " The Critic " was
brought out in 1779. His last work, largely
a translation from Kotzebue, was " Pizarro "
(1779).

Sheridan was at different times a member of
Parliament, an under-secretary of state and
secretary of treasury. It was Sheridan that
conducted the attack in the celebrated
Warren-Hastings trial. Famous as an orator

and writer, reckless in his manner of life, ruined by the burning of Drury Lane, he died in poverty and distress in 1816, and was buried in Westminster Abbey.

Besides the plays already mentioned, Sheridan was the author of a popular farce, "St. Patrick's Day," and an opera (music by Linley, Sheridan's father-in-law), "The Duenna," both produced in 1775. "The Duenna" combines the merits of legitimate comedy with the attractions of poetry and song, and was so successful as to be given seventy-five times at Convent Garden during the season.

It is remarkable that many of our best comedies have been written by very young men. All of Congreve's plays were written before he was twenty-five. Farquhar died at the age of twenty-nine. Vanbrugh was only a youth when he planned "The Relapse." Sheridan wrote "The Rivals" at the age of twenty-four, and "The School for Scandal" at twenty-six.

However, the latter play had been long contemplated, and was altered and rewritten a number of times previous to its production, the part of Sir Peter Teasle having been a rather late addition. The principal merit of the play lies neither in the

rather slender plot nor in any sympathy we
have for the characters, but rather in the
strikingly natural situations, the skillful handling of the piece, the constantly brilliant wit,
the animation, the sense of the ridiculous and
the finish given to the whole. The comedy is
a triumph of art, and its merit is only exceeded
by its popularity. It has been translated into
most of the languages of Europe.

"The Critic," still occasionally given, is an
excellent farce, written on the model of Vil-
lier's famous "Rehearsal."

Thompson's successful translation from the
German of "The Stranger," in 1798, induced
Sheridan to a like attempt. In 1779, therefore, "Pizarro" (from Kotzebue's play) was
brought out at Drury Lane. The heroic interest of the story, and the splendor of the
production, made it popular, but, as a literary
achievement, it detracted rather than added
to Sheridan's fame.

The ill-treatment which OLIVER GOLD-
SMITH (1728–1774) received at the hands of
London managers undoubtedly dampened
the ardor of one of the drama's most gifted
votaries. Garrick looked coldly on his first
play, "The Good-Natured Man," and "She
Stoops to Conquer" met with but little favor

at he hands of the elder Colman, who produced it only under protest, March 15th, 1773. In consequence of the reception accorded him by critics and managers, Goldsmith gave up writing for the stage. He was born in 1728, of Irish parents, in straightened circumstances, and was educated at Trinity College, Dublin. He led an adventurer's life in England and on the continent ; acquired fame as poet and dramatist, and died in 1774. He was buried in the yard of Temple Church, but has a monument in Westminster Abbey.

GEORGE COLMAN, the younger (1762–1836) belongs equally to the latter half of the eighteenth and the first half of the nineteenth century. He may justly be considered as the connecting link between these two periods, but as his best works were written before 1800, and as his memory is so intimately connected with that of Garrick, Sheridan, etc., we will speak of him here. Both the elder and younger Colman were actors, managers and authors, the son excelling his father, however, in the last named capacity. The younger Colman's first play, "The Female Dramatist (1782), a farce, was a failure. His second, " Two to One " (1784), a comedy, was more succesful. " Inkle and Yarico " (1787),

" Way and Means " (1788), " The Iron Chest "
(1796), a poetic melodrama ; " The Heir-at-
Law " (1797), " The Poor Gentleman " (1800),
and " John Bull " (1802), were all excellent
productions, and became established favorites,
though one of them, " The Iron Chest," was
not favorably received on its first performance. Colman's best work was undoubtedly
his comedy, " The Heir-at-Law," which may
be ranked amongst the finest of its kind in
our dramatic literature. It still holds the
stage, and its popularity continues undimin-
ished. This is largely due to the highly
amusing and original character of the learned
tutor, Dr. Pangloss. About 1798 Colman
became interested in spectacular pieces and
pantomine, and before 1800 had produced
" Blue Beard," " Children in the Wood,"
" Obi," etc.

O'Keefe's " Wild Oats," Morton's " Speed
the Plow," and Cumberland's " The West
Indian," all meritorious comedies, belong to
the close of the eighteenth century.

VI.

THE NINETEENTH CENTURY.

IT is with extreme diffidence that I approach the concluding chapter of my work.
To deal with affairs of the remote past is
usually a safe undertaking. For here time
has furnished landmarks to guide and records
to confirm the student in his assertions.
But the nearer he approaches the present,
the more unstable does he find his supports
and the fewer his authorities. Till at last
he is forced boldly to draw his own
conclusions from given facts, and look to the
world for that approval or rejection of his
statements, which he can find nowhere else.
It is unfortunately true that it is well-nigh
impossible to view the present with an impartial eye, and the historian of his own time
is invariably unjust to some one. It is only
after a certain time has elapsed, when our
sympathies have ceased to be so warm that
they blind our judgment, that we can com-
ment with fairness. It is this predicament in

which I find myself. Though much that I have to treat of is sufficiently remote to be handled safely, yet in attempting to bring my subject down to the present there is a great deal of which I must speak, whose treatment by me may be censured. I trust, however, that my zeal and my desire to be just may steer me safely past the rocks which beset the pilot in comparatively unexplored seas.

We have said the year 1800 found the stage in possession of a brilliant comedy, a mediocre tragedy, a picturesque melodrama, and an infant opera. Original comedy after Tobin's " Honeymoon," and one or two final productions of Colman's gave way to the farces of Poole and Planché for some twenty years. Then appeared the greatest dramatist of his age, JAMES SHERIDAN KNOWLES, who enriched comedy and tragedy alike, and whose works, though considered a trifle old-fashioned and theatrical to-day, nevertheless continue to hold the stage and the public heart. Knowles returned boldly to blank verse in his comedies, and was eminently successful in a rather hazardous undertaking. For verse had long been confined to serious and prose assigned to lighter efforts. Nor was he less successful in tragedy. Being an actor, his works were better plays than those of his immediate predecessors in this field, Joanna Baillie, Walter Savage Landor and Henry Hart Milman. Nor did his works suffer by comparison with such contemporaries as Byron, De Vere and Lytton, though he can not be said to have equaled in poetic merit at least Browning. Indeed the drama may be said to have experienced a comparatively brilliant florescence during the thirty years included between 1820 and 1850.

The nineteenth century's first score of years had been, in a dramatic way, uneventful, broken only here and there by an entertaining comedy, or a passable tragedy, the greater number of plays given being, however, farces by Poole or Planché, or revivals of former successes. This was due, no doubt, largely to the wars in which Great Britain was engaged with France and America. With peace sprang up a coterie of vigorous and gifted play-wrights. This second dramatic period beheld the production of such comedies as "The Hunchback," "Love," "The Love Chase," "London Assurance," and such tragedies as "Virginius," "Richelieu," "Rienzi," "Damon and Pythias," "Werner," and "Blot in the 'Scutcheon." By the side of the more pronounced dramatic types, and between them, appeared the domestic, the " Robertson," comedy, or what might be called, for so it in time has come to be, the comedy-drama.

With the retirement of Knowles, and the death of several of his distinguished contemporaries, dramatic poetry perceptibly waned. Comedy returned once more to prose, and tragedy, save as a literary exotic, ceased to exist. From time to time some great poet writes a tragedy—for the library. It seldom reaches the stage. Tennyson's attempts have not been successful. Browning, belonging to an earlier period, was, even in his own time, only partially so. To-day the tragedy of the past engrosses the stage—and yet not wholly so. An American poet has arisen who has already enriched our stage with two excellent works, "Pendragon" and "Ganelon." Let us hope that Mr. Younge's efforts are only a promise of what is to come.

1850–1890 represents a period of great productivity, if not of surpassing merit. Scott, Dickens, Twain and other successful novelists have had their works contorted in ruthless dramatizations. The French, German and lately the Scandinavian drama has been translated and adapted. Brougham's burlesques and Gilbert's poetic fantasies have appeared. Comic opera has sprung into wonderful popularity. For a time French sensationalism held the boards. This gave way to the combined forces of the English melodrama, the German farce and the American comedy-drama in its various forms. Prior to 1850 America could lay little claim to an indigenous drama. Whatever was meritorious was imported, and the theatre was provincial. Brougham's " Pocahontas," in 185-, was the signal for the awakening of a native drama. Gradually the development has gone on, until to-day America boasts a host of vigorous and ambitious play-wrights. We point with pride to the names of Howard, Mackaye, Young, Campbell, and count amongst the best productions, " The Danites," " My Partner," " The Banker's Daughter," " The Henrietta," " Shenandoah," " Ganelon," " The Wife " and " The Senator." To-day America not merely imports, but exchanges dramatic commodities.

The century was ushered in, as we have mentioned before, by Colman's " The Poor Gentleman," presently followed by " John Bull," both excellent comedies.

In 1804 that unfortunate dramatist, JOHN

TOBIN (1770-1804), who had spent the best part of his life writing plays, only to have them rejected, died. Shortly afterwards his comedy, "The Honeymoon," was produced, with what favor is well known. The play is by no means a perfect one, showing, indeed, a lamentable lack of originality, but its popularity has been ever considerable. There is an undeniable air of imitation to a half dozen standard plays, but the imitations are so cleverly executed that the whole may well be said to constitute a new work.

JOANNA BAILLIE, WALTER SAVAGE LANDOR, and HENRY HART MILMAN are the names which represent whatever of merit was achieved in the field of tragedy during the first twenty years of this century. None of them experienced great success in the representation of their works, though Milman's "Fazio" was favorably received at Convent Garden in 1815, and several of Miss Baillie's plays were produced and approved before critical audiences. Landor's "Count Julian" (1812), while a magnificent poem, is deficient in ease and continuity, and quite unfit for presentation. Miss Baillie wrote a series of plays illustrative of the passions, as "De Montfort," a tragedy on Hatred, and "Basil," a tragedy on Love. Her object, undoubtedly a highly moral one, was to picture the beginnings, progress and results of a passion. Even with John Kemble and Mrs. Siddons in the leading roles her plays did not become popular, showing the great disadvantage a writer, however gifted, labors under when not acquainted with the requirements of the stage.

JOHN POOLE (1786–1872), and JAMES ROBINSON PLANCHÉ (1796–1880), are the two names most intimately acquainted with the farce and light comedy of the first half of the nineteenth century. The best known works of the former are his " Hamlet Travestie " (1810), " Paul Pry," a farce, (1825), and " Patrician and Parvenu," a comedy (1835). Poole lived to an advanced age, dying almost for‧gotten. Planché composed more than two hundred pieces for the stage of the lightest possible description. In 1818 his burlesque " Amorosa, or King of Little Britian," was produced successfully at Drury Lane. In 1828 appeared his fifty-fifth and best play, " Charles XII." In addition to his dramatic efforts he has published fairy tales, romances, and a history of British costumes (1834).

We have said that amongst the dramatists

of the latter half of the eighteenth century, Sheridan shone forth resplendently ; that by his brilliancy he obscured the merits of his fellows. In a somewhat less degree the same statement is applicable in his time, the first half of the nineteenth century, to JAMES SHERIDAN KNOWLES (1784–1862). Certain it is that in the sustaining of dramatic interest and poetic value, and at the same time in obtaining popular approval, he excels his contemporaries, however he may fall below them at any particular point.

Knowles was born in Cork, Ireland. He was the son of James Knowles, who was the nephew of Thomas Sheridan, therefore a cousin of Richard Brinsley Sheridan. James Knowles was an elocution teacher and an author of a Pronouncing English Dictionary. His son at the age of twelve wrote plays for the amusement of his companions and himself. At twenty-two young Knowles became an actor. At thirty-one he produced Caius Gracchus " (1815), a tragedy, in Belfast, Ireland. In 1820, with Macready in the title role, "Virginius" was brought out at Convent Garden, and James Sheridan Knowles became one of the leading play-wrights in England. In the following twenty years he produced at one or another of the leading London theatres the historical play, "Alfred the Great" (1831), the tragedy "John of Procida" (1840), and the comedies, under which head we group all his other works : "William Tell" (1825), "The Hunchback" (1833), "The Wife" (1833), "The Beggar of Bethnal Green" (1834), "The Daughter" (1836), "The Love Chase" (1837), "Love" (1837), "Woman's Wit" (1838), "The Maid of Mariendorpt" (1838), "Old Maids" (1841), "The Rose of Aragon" (1842), and "The Secretary" (184-).

His plays had the advantage of such interpreters as Macready, Charles Kean and Ellen Tree. In "The Hunchback" and "The Wife" he assumed the leading roles, playing Master Walter in the former, and Julian St. Pierre in the latter.

He made a successful tour of the United States before abandoning the stage, which he did in 1845. He became a Baptist minister and novelist. Several sermons attest the first fact and two novels, "George Lovel" and "Henry Fortescue," the latter. In 1849 he was granted a pension of £200, which protected his old age from want.

Knowles excels undoubtedly in his love

scenes.   He has an infinite amount of tenderness, a high conception of the marriage rela-
tion, a noble morality, considerable humor and
no small fund of pathos.   He is in sympathy
with the human heart and its emotions, and
consequently will receive popular approval
always.   His poetry is smooth, elegant, and
often beautiful. His verse is somewhat monotonous, though always pleasing. He is at times
too wordy.   His knowledge of stage-effect is
constantly visible, in fact in places uncom-
fortably so, for it has caused a theatrical
coloring that is not at all times pleasant.

I have before had occasion to speak of a
man raised to celebrity in dramatic literature
by a single play. Somewhat more than a
century after Addison's "Cato," appeared
JOHN BANIM'S (1798–1842) tragedy of "Damon
and Pythias."   The play, with Macready and
Kemble in the leading roles, met with the
warmest enthusiasm.   It rewarded its young
Irish author (Banim was only in his twenty-
fourth year) with fame, which he unfortunately did nothing more to deserve   He died
in poverty, a government pension being his
chief support in his last years.

To that class of writers whose works belong
wholly to the library, we must assign SIR

AUBREY DE VERE (1788–1846), the Irish poet. His works contain three poetical historical dramas, "Julian, the Apostate" (1822), "The Duke of Mercia" (1823), and "Mary Tudor" (1844). They are of no particular merit.

MARY RUSSELL MITFORD (1786–1855) is an authoress of several excellent plays, one at least of sufficient merit to commend it to a tragedian of our own day. Her blank-verse dramas include "Julian" (1823), "Foscari" (1826), "Rienzi" (1828), "Charles I.," and a number of others. "Rienzi," a powerful if somewhat gloomy tragedy, is the best and most popular of her works.

That erratic poet, GEORGE GORDON, LORD BYRON (1788–1824), has left several dramas, three of which are tragedies, and one he called a mystery play. "The Two Foscari," an historical tragedy (1821), was intended not to be acted, but to be read. Like "Sardanapalus," "The Two Foscari" is a success neither as a poem nor as a play ; being too heavy and dull for the one, and too verbose and ill-constructed for the other. His plays are too solemn and lacking in action to be favorites on the stage. They were most severely criticized on their appearance. "Werner" (1822) alone proved successful in representation. And this play Lord Byron, having abandoned the classical unities, stated expressly was not suited or prepared for the stage. "Cain," except in topic, has little resemblance to the old Mystery Plays. "The Deformed Transformed" (1821) is a feeble variation of the old Faustus legend. "Werner" was successfully revived by Henry Irving in recent years.

DOUGLAS WILLIAM JERROLD (1803–1857) was successively sailor, printer, author and manager. His first comedy, "More Frightened than Hurt," was written at the age of fifteen. It remained unread in the desk of a London manager for two years, when it was perused and produced successfully at Sadler's Wells, in 1821. "Black-Eyed Susan," a nautical play, brought out in 1829, at the Surrey Theatre, ran for over three hundred nights, although its author received but seventy pounds for it. Amongst his other plays may be mentioned "The Devil's Ducat," "The Rent Day," "Nell Gwynne" and "Beau Nash." In 1841 Jerrold became a contributor to *Punch*, where his "Caudle Lectures" brought him considerable fame.

EDWARD BULWER LYTTON (1805–1873). Lord Lytton, best known as a novelist, made his

first attempt at dram ic writing in 1836,
when he produced " T e Duchess de Val-
lière," which failed. His subsequent plays,
" The Lady of Lyons," " Richelieu " and
" Money," were highly successful, and are
still frequently g ven by our actors of the
" legitimate." Though the blank verse of
" The Lady of Lyons " ard " Richelieu " is
somewhat florid, the charac rs and situations
are strong and dramatic, and, in the hands of
talented actors, extremely ef ective.

Special mention should be made of a
manager whose enterprise was so great that
instead of yielding his theatre t
of foreign plays, or adaptation
novels, encouraged and fost   ds,
effort by producing annually   ne he
BENJAMIN WEBSTER, himself an
some merit, became manager   ay-
market Theatre in 1837. He brought out
at great expense the plays of Bulwer,
Knowles, Jerrold, and others, and dramatic literature owes not a little to his liberal
management.   At his theatre, Macready,
Wallack, Farren, Miss Faucit and other
famous actors appeared.

Our century has beheld a single Elizabethan
dramatic poet, and it has not proved itself

worthy of him. ROBERT BROWNING (1812–
1889) possessed all (the genius and more of
the refinement necessary to place his name
amongst our great dramatists of the Shakespearean era. He lacked, unfortunately,
their practical knowledge of the stage. Also
it is to be regretted that in the age in which
he wrote the theatre was sought less for in-
struction than entertainment, and poetic
plays to be attractive had also to be theatrical. His psychological studies, however they
might be appreciated to-day, were entirely
unsuited for his audiences of forty years ago.
F   poets have reasoned so well in
               such tenderness, such a delicate
an   right and wrong.
in   182   in the 'Scutcheon " (1843) we
               t perfect drama ; all the fire and
gen   Elizabethan, softened and refined,
however by our nineteenth century philosophy. The very youthful age of the heroine
Mildred, is a defect, undoubtedly, but such a
defect as a greater poet than Browning is guilty
of. This but serves, however, to display more
fully the other beauties of the piece. There
is nothing of its kind more lovely than Mer-
ton's serenade. " The Blot in the 'Scutcheon "
was produced in 1843 at Drury Lane, Lon-

don ; afterwards played with some success in the United States by Lawrence Barrett.

Of Browning's plays, "Pauline" and "Paracelsus" were published before 1837, in which year his tragedy "Stafford" failed in representation. "Pippa Passes" appeared in 1841 ; "King Victor and King Charles" (1842) ; "The Return of the Druses" and "A Blot in the 'Scutcheon" (1843) ; "Colombe's Birthday (1844) ; "Luria" and "A Soul's Tragedy" (1845).

JOHN BALDWIN BUCKSTONE (1802–1879) was a well-known actor and dramatist both in England and America. His plays,, mostly comedies and farces, number more than two hundred, many of which are still great favorites. The most famous are "Married Life," "Single Life," "Rough Diamond," "Good for Nothing," "Flowers of the Forest," "Irish Lion" and "Jack Sheppherd."

JOHN BROUGHAM (1810–1880) adds one more name to the list of clever Irish play-wrights. Brougham was intended for the medical profession, but became an actor, first in London, afterwards in America. During his career he managed a theatre in Boston and two in New York ; the Bowery (1856–7), and Brougham's Lyceum, afterwards Wallacks (1850–2).

The latter he built, but surrendered the management of after two seasons. He was the author of various comedies, dramas and extravaganzas, the most celebrated of which are " Pocahontas," " Romance and Reality," " My Cousin German," " Dombey and Son " (dramatization), and " Bleak House " (dramatization.) He also published books of stories under the titles of " A Basket of Chips," and " The Bunsby Papers."

DION BOUCICAULT (1822–   ) was born in Dublin, where his father, a French refugee, was a merchant. Upon being sent to London to be educated as a civil engineer, he became instead a dramatist and actor. In 1841 his first and probably his best comedy, " London Assurance," was produced successfully at Convent Garden, London. He devoted himself to literature and the stage, and has written, during his long and prosperous career, upward of one hundred pieces. The plots of Boucicault's plays are seldom original. His excellence as a dramatist consists rather in action and dialogue, which is always clever and often novel. His melodramas and his Irish characters are a vast improvement on their predecessors in these fields. In fact, Boucicault has elevated them by introducing a life, interest and naturalness they did not possess before. His constructive power and knowledge of stage effect is of the best. A list of Dion Boucicault's popular pieces will include " The Corsican Brothers," " The Willow Copse," " Jessie Brown," Colleen Bawn," " Arrah-na-Pogue," " The Long Strike," " Hunted Down," " Rip Van Winkle," " Peep O'Day," " The Shaugran," " Led Astray " and " The Jilt." As an actor Boucicault's fame rests chiefly on the portrayal of eccentric and Irish characters. He has written, besides his plays, many newspaper articles on dramatic subjects. It is largely due to his influence that dramatists are to-day properly remunerated, which they were not at the beginning of this century.

A prolific and popular play-wright, one who, in his day, ranked amongst the best, was TOM TAYLOR (1817–1880). As a student at college he distinguished himself by carrying off gold medals, prizes and the highest honors, and he became a fellow of Cambridge. After leaving his Alma Mater, he was for two years Professor of English Literature at University College, London. He studied law, contributed to the papers, and before 1850 became a noted author. Like some others of his contemporaries he excelled in the number rather than the originality of his works, having produced, alone or in conjunction with others, more than one hundred pieces. His greatest desire in constructing a play, was that it should act well. In this he was usually successful, his knowledge of the stage and its demands being of great service to him. His language, though never surprisingly brilliant, is effective. His characters are natural and consistent. His blank verse historical dramas, as " 'Twixt Axe and Crown " (1870), are not so successful as his other works. " The Ticket of Leave Man," a version of " Le Retour de Melun "; " Lady Clancarty " (1874), an original play ; " The Fool's Revenge," from Victor Hugo's " Le Roi s'amuse " (same subject as Verdi's " Rigoletto ") ; " Our American Cousin," a play with a peculiar history (a minor part was raised to such prominence by a clever actor as to forever overshadow all the rest) ; " Still Waters Run Deep," " The Overland Route," " An Unequal Match," are amongst Taylor's best known dramas.

THOMAS WILLIAM ROBERTSON (1829–1871) has given his name to what is known as the " Robertson " comedy, as being its most fitting exponent, and, indeed to a degree, its originator. His works are serious comedies, or what we to-day call comedy-dramas ; plays in which the light and shade is equally mingled, where the affairs treated of are of everyday occurrence, the people such as we see around us, and the conclusion usually a happy one, the idea of the whole being to impress some moral lesson or discuss some social question. Robertson was for a time an actor in his father's company, a travelling one. In 1851 his first piece, " A Night's Adventure," was produced. In 1860 Robertson settled in London, and wrote his series of dramas to which he owes his fame : " David Garrick," " Society," " Ours," " Caste," " Play," " School," " M. P." and " War."

Of those play-wrights who have been influenced by the Robertson comedies, H. J. BYRON and A. W. PINERO are the most conspicuous. Byron was more inclined to farcial elements than Robertson, and made his most lasting success with " Our Boys " (1878). Pinero has shown a more serious tendency, and his plays are superior to those of his master, revealing a strength in which Robertson is lacking. Pinero's chief merit, the proper harmony between action and dialogue, has been taught him, no doubt, as an actor. "The Money Spinner," "Sweet Lavender" and "The Weaker Sex," are the works by which he has acquired his enviable reputation.

From the early part of the century the meretricious habit of supplying the deficiency of dramatic material by dramatizing celebrated novels, had been growing in popularity, until it threatened to put a stop to all original effort. The works of Scott, Dickens, Lytton, Mrs. Henry Wood and others were hacked, twisted and mutilated for stage purposes. This lamentable practice has prevailed even to our day. It is rare that a novel, however dramatic, contains more than an idea for a good play, and the book invariably suffers by the dramatization, while the stage seldom gains anything by the transaction. However, the celebrity of a widely-read novel conduces largely to increase the receipts of a play taken from it, and managers of the last fifty years have often found it profitable to produce such plays. Amongst those novelists whose pens as well as books have contributed to the stage, are CHARLES READE and WILKIE COLLINS. The works of both may be termed sensational, yet, undoubtedly containing many excellencies. Reade and Taylor's joint work, " Masks and Faces " (1854), and Reade's dramatization of Zola's " L'Assommoir," which he called "Drink" (1879), are his chief claims to remembrance.   WILKIE COLLINS'S plays were all taken from his famous novels.   Though severely criticized, they attained considerable popularity and contain much good material. " The New Magdalen," " Man and Wife " and " The Woman in White," are his best known works.

Dramatic poetry, whose chief aim is literary, and which has rarely succeeded in representation, has never been without its supporters throughout the century.   JOANNA BAILLIE, LANDOR, MILMAN, DE VERE, BYRON, BROWNING, SWINBURNE, TENNYSON, form a chain of names extending over a period of ninety years from 1800 to 1890.   Some of them never produced, though they published their works, and none of them achieved any considerable popularity as dramatists.

ALGERNON CHARLES SWINBURNE (1837–   ) presents the to-day rather unusual spectacle of an English poet modeling his efforts on the Greeks ; and what is still more unusual, successfully.   Swinburne is a poet, in speaking

of whom a commentator is obliged to judge
for himself, so diverse are the opinions of
critics.   His admirers being excessive in their
praise, and his enemies in their detraction ;
making the one appear adulation and the
other abuse.   In 1865 Swinburne achieved
fame by the publishing of his classical tragedy
" Atalanta in Calydon," a unique and admirable effort.   In 1876 " Erechtheus," a second
classical drama, appeared.   The dramatic
trilogy in which the Queen of Scots is condemned by the poet, " Chastelard " (1865),
" Bothwell " (1874), and " Mary Stuart "
(1881), is particularly interesting.   " Marino
Faliero "(1885), is perhaps superior to Byron's
tragedy on the same subject.   " The Queen
Mother," " Rosamond," appeared in 1860.
" Locrine " in 1887.

ALFRED, LORD TENNYSON (1809-   ), com-
pletes the above list of dramatic poets.   He
is the representative of the poetry of his age,
the Victorian.   No one of this century has
equaled him in popularity and prosperity in
his own province.   It is unnecessary to speak
of the manifold beauties of his verse since
they are known so well throughout the Eng-
lish-reading world.   It is sufficient for our
purpose here to say that his best efforts are

not his plays, though they have not detracted from his reputation. They comprise " Queen Mary " (1875), " Harold " (1877), " The Falcon " (1879), " The Cup " (1881), " The Promise of May " (1882), " Becket " (1884).

The most brilliant satirist and humorist of the century is unquestionably WILLIAM SCHWENK GILBERT (1836–   ). Notwithstanding that he was educated for a barrister and admitted to the bar, he devoted himself to literature, later especially to play-writing. His fairy comedies " The Palace of Truth " (1870), " Pygmalion and Galathea " (1871), " The Wicked World " (1873), and " Broken Hearts " (1876), met with unusual and deserved success. One of his cleverest works is a burlesque comedy, " Engaged " (1877), which is as scintillating with wit as it is pointed in satire. In 1878 appeared " Ne'er do Well," a farce. Subsequently Mr. Gilbert has applied his energies to supplying the librettos for that very popular series of comic operas, " Pinafore," " The Pirates of Penzance," " Patience," " Iolanthe," " Mikado," " Yeoman of the Guard," " The Gondoliers," etc. In November, 1883, Miss Mary Anderson produced at the Lyceum Theatre, London, the play upon which Mr. Gilbert's claim to excellence will probably be judged, "Comedy and Tragedy." This remarkable little drama comprehends in one act all the various shades of comedy and tragedy, and is highly effective, from both a literary and dramatic point of view. Although open to criticism on historical grounds, it is nevertheless one of the most important contributions of the decade. "Comedy and Tragedy" is its author's chief serious attempt. His first work was "Dulcimara" (1866).

We have spoken already of the fashion that grew up of transforming the novel into the play, and of the impediment it became to original effort. But this was not the only discouragement the young dramatist of that time, 1860 to 1880, encountered in London. Not only did the manager find it safer and more profitable to produce a version of some popular novel than an untried play, but likewise was it discovered what a profitable investment an adapted or translated Parisian success was. Although the custom of producing such plays was an ancient one, it had never been so remunerative. The result was that for a score of years foreign plays held the stage of the best London theatres, just as they did so long the New York theatres. It was held to be folly to risk money on the production of a native play, whose attractive power was uncertain, when favorite continental plays might be obtained, whose popularity was in a measure secured. During this period were introduced in England, chiefly by adaptations, in America by translations, the works of DUMAS, SCRIBE, D'ENNERRY, SARDOU, etc. The most famous of these plays being "Adrienne L'Ecouvre," "Camille," "The Two Orphans," "A Scrap of Paper," "Diplomacy," "Fedora."

The eagerness with which the public accepted these Gallic productions drew attention to the advantages and embellishments of the French drama, and to the opportunities France and her people offer for dramatic study. English writers began to choose French subjects and French scenes and characters. The most excellent of these compositions, in fact one of the best plays of the age, is Merivale and Grove's "Forget-Me-Not," produced August 21st, 1879, at the Lyceum Theatre, London, by Miss Genevieve Ward. The *Saturday Review,* of August the 13th, 1879, has this to say of the above-mentioned play :

" ' Forget-Me-Not ' has, in a marked degree, the combined strength and brightness which belongs to the best examples of the contemporary French drama, and it has the advantage of not turning on conjugal infidelity. The leading idea of the piece is entirely new ; the construction is good, and the dialogue is pointed, brilliant and natural."

Like all successful efforts, it has had a host of inferior imitators.

Another dramatic sensation, and, in a way, an important event, was the appearance about this time of " The Danites," by Joaquin Miller. A well-written, genuine American play was a most agreeable novelty. A number of plays, extravagant in characters and absurd or improbable in theme, such as " The Gilded Age " and "The Mighty Dollar," had served as vehicles for the peculiar talents of some celebrated actor, but had never deserved the name of American Plays. " The Danites " supplied this deficiency. It is a melodrama, full of attractive freshness and novelty, telling a story of human interest, and picturing naturally a life peculiar to our pioneer civilization.

What has been said in this lecture will apply, in a general way, to the American as well as the English theatre. America, prior to 1850, had no drama ; and with the spirit

and dash characteristic of the land, has
endeavored to accomplish in forty years what
has taken England three centuries. So well
has she succeeded, that, though we have no
great dramatic poets as yet, we have attempted,
with moderate success, the various phases of
the play, and are to-day sending our dramas
to London, and having them translated into
foreign languages. A short sketch of our
leading New York stock theatres will give the
best possible idea of what has been done for
the drama in this country.

In 1852 Brougham's Lyceum passed into
the hands of James Wallack, and became
known as Wallack's Lyceum. In time a new
house was built, and the name Wallack's alone
was retained. Under the management of
James Wallack, and afterwards of his son
Lester, Wallack's Theatre was the standard
for all that was best in the dramatic line in
the United States. Particularly were the old
comedy productions famous. Unfortunately
the theatre did not keep apace with the times,
and in the eighties began to lose its position.
The cause was undoubtedly its persistent
loyalty to England, to which country it
looked almost exclusively for its plays, many
of which, when produced, were neither meri-

torious nor popular. In 1889 the company ceased to exist, and the theatre, which was at that time its home, became a " combination " house.

For many years Augustin Daly has been a prominent manager of New York at different theatres. His early management was marked by the production of translations from the French, such as " Frou-Frou," and some English and American plays. For about eleven years Mr. Daly has occupied the pretty little theatre on Broadway and Thirtieth Street, known as Daly's, which he has made the home of the leading comedy company of the country. His productions have consisted of adaptations from the best French and German farce comedies, and in revivals of the comedies of Shakespeare and the Restoration dramatists. His most successful revivals have been " The Merry Wives of Windsor," " The Taming of the Shrew," " The Midsummer Night's Dream," " As You Like It," " The Country Girl," " The Inconstant," and "She Would and She Would Not."

Mr. A. M. Palmer, whose name is so intimately connected with the Union Square Theatre of the past, and the Madison Square

Theatre of the present, has the reputation of having produced fewer failures than any manager in America. The Union Square, under Mr. Palmer's management saw the successful production of M. Feuillet's " Tentation," and " Un-Roman Parisien "; D'Ennerry's " The Two Orphans "; Bronson Howard's " Banker's Daughter "; Bartley Campbell's " My Partner " ; Sardou's " Andrea " and " Daniel Rochat " ; Belot and Nus' " Miss Multon " and " The Danicheffs," " The Celebrated Case," " Rose Michel," etc., etc. The Madison Square Theatre, under its first management, was given up exclusively to the production of plays by American dramatists. Here appeared Steele Mackaye's " Hazel Kirke "; Mrs. Burnett and W. H. Gillette's " Esmeralda "; and Bronson Howard's " Young Mrs. Winthrop." Under Mr. Palmer's management we have seen the English successes " Jim, The Penman," " Captain Swift " and " Aunt Jack " ; also the native plays " Sealed Instructions " and " Elaine."

The Lyceum Theatre has continued the policy inaugurated by the Madison Square. Here have been presented Howard's " One of Our Girls " ; De Mille and Belasco's " The

Wife" and "The Charity Ball"; and Belasco's "Lord Chumley."

To-day the metropolitan theatres of England and America present a singularly cosmo-
politan appearance. But not only may the
drama in its various phases of nationality be
observed in the same evening, but also in the
different stages of its development. English,
American, French, German, Italian; even
Chinese plays have been given almost
simultaneously. To-night (March, 1890), may
be seen in the city of New York Shakespearean tragedy, Shakespearean comedy,
farce-comedy, French melodrama, American
comedy-drama, an American farce, an American comedy, two American rural plays, an
American military drama, German grand
opera, German comic opera, German comedy,
German tragedy, American melodrama, one
of Sheridan's comedies, an English comic
opera, an English melodrama and an English comedy-drama.

FINIS.

REFERENCES.

1. Sharpe's "Coventry Mysteries."
2. "The York Plays," Lucy Toulman Smith.
3. Ward's "History of English Dramatic Literature."
4. Collier's "Annals of the Stage."
5. Dodsley's Old Plays.
6. Doran's "Annals of the Stage."
7. "Shakespeare's Predecessors in the English Drama," John Addington Symonds.
8. "Shakespeare's Complete Works," G. L. Duyckinck.
9. Augustus Wilhelm Schlegel's "Dramatic Art and Literature."
10. H. A. Taine's "History of English Literature."
11. S. T. Coleridge's "Notes and Lectures on Shakespeare."
12. H. Ulrici's "Shakespeare's Dramatic Art."
13. The Works of Jonson, Beaumont and Fletcher, Ford, Webster, Marston, Dekker, Massinger, Middleton, Heywood, Shirley, etc., etc.

14. " Life of David Garrick."
15. " Memoirs of the Coleman Family," R. B. Peake.
16. " Life of Sheridan," Thos. Moore.
17. Mrs. Inchbold's " British Theatre."
18. The Works of Congreve, Wycherly, Farquhar, Vanbrugh, Centlivre, Etherege, Otway, Davenant, Lillo, Foote, O'-Keefe, Cumberland, Colman, Goldsmith, Sheridan, Knowles, etc., etc., etc.
19. The Works of Baillie, Milman, Mitford, Byron, DeVere, Browning, Swinburne, Tennyson, Knowles, Boucicault, Merivale, Howard, etc., etc.
20. " The Saturday Review," London (1869–1889).
21. " The New York Clipper."
22. " The Theatres."